FUCK AGING

FUCK
AGING

Live a Kick-Ass Second Half

KATHLEEN E. SINCLAIR

LIONCREST
PUBLISHING

FUCK AGING
Live a Kick-Ass Second Half

ISBN   978-1-5445-2888-5 *Hardcover*

978-1-5445-2889-2 *Paperback*

978-1-5445-2890-8 *Ebook*

978-1-5445-3165-6 *Audiobook*

CONTENTS

*To the mentors I have had in my life,
starting with my grandmother, T.T., when I was four
years old. Thank you for believing in me and showing me
the exit when I would get lost on the highway
of procrastination and doubt.*

INTRODUCTION

Okay, I might as well address the big OMG in the room now so we can get on with it. What was I thinking with a title like *Fuck Aging*? You might be saying, "Isn't that illegal or something? How can I have a book with that title on my bedside table? What will people think? I will have to wrap it in brown paper. We're not supposed to say that word, are we?"

And that is my point. People tell us what to wear, think, eat, exercise, do, and say just because we are "older." First of all, they lump everyone from fifty or sixty to holy-shit old into the same group. Well, that's like saying someone who is twenty is just like someone who is sixty. I don't think so.

As I have learned, and as I hope you will too, you have to let all of that misguided advice go, like pasta water through a sieve, leaving only the good stuff. And the good stuff is the authentic you. Let the bad stuff wash over you and go down the drain.

But the thing that clinched the title for me was when I was hanging out with a bunch of friends (yes, maybe there was wine) and we were talking about people saying, "You don't look your age."

Now, I know that is supposed to be some kind of compliment, but really, what the hell does it mean? Based on what? Did I miss the memo about what I was supposed to look like at a certain age? Does a comparison hologram magically pop up and, oops, yes you do look good for your age? Did you get that memo? And I want to say "good compared to who?" Your Aunt Mildred or Uncle Louie or maybe your neighbor or that movie star. Where is this coming from? Anyway, the wine was flowing and we were falling off our chairs laughing and comparing notes when we all said, at the same time, "Fuck aging." How could I not honor that sweet revelation? But I digress.

Ask yourself if you are ordinary, wishy-washy, or wimpy. Are you happy just taking up space? Of course not, because if you were, you wouldn't be reading this book! Especially not with that title.

This book is *not* for people who don't want to change. It will be confrontational, challenging, and direct. It has a lot of swear words, plus it asks you to do a shit ton of hard work. You have to do the work; it is a must. You will get shaken, stirred, and hung out to dry. The good news is that you are only one book (this book) away from a totally different life and way of living over sixty! Or any age at which you want to start over, actually.

People over sixty often feel discouraged and brushed aside. They feel they aren't respected, and they definitely feel they're not heard. Many people have told me they feel invisible. Add that to the anxiety about whether they will be able to afford healthcare or have money for other things they need and you end up with a gloomy future.

This book will address many ways to gain respect, be heard, and make a difference. It will show you how to get organized, maximize your time, and use the knowledge you have to move forward and find a new purpose for living and helping others. You will read the stories of people who have struggled with some of the same issues you are facing and learn how they stayed motivated to reach their goals.

Anything worth doing requires movement and change. I have lived a long life. As I write this book, I am seventy-six years young. But it wasn't until I put in the work around age sixty that my life shifted. I am now living a kick-ass second half of my life, and I couldn't be happier. Or wait, maybe I could be... There is always more work to be done.

Let me tell you that when I started this journey, I had no idea what I was doing or how to figure it out. I remember reading something about standing on the shoulders of giants and how it is wise to learn from people who are already successful. How did they do it?

Well, I went to seminars, workshops, and lectures. I joined mastermind groups with really smart people. I became a member of various organizations and worked hard to learn as much as I could. I also gained an entire bookshelf of new books.

When I figured out my purpose about five years ago, I took classes on how to become a speaker and gave little talks at Toastmasters. I read books on how to write books and took classes on that too. I set up a website and wrote tons of articles and blog posts about challenging aging, and I traveled and met many people.

All along the way, I gained the skills I needed to connect with people over sixty and start a movement that would change the way we look at aging and shift from a negative attitude about growing older to one of possibility and fulfillment.

I realized, through my hard work, my travels, and the people I met around the world, that many people my age or sixty-plus weren't living a full life. They seemed to have given up or to have given in to "getting old." I just couldn't stand by and not share my lessons, the work I had done and continue to do, and watch people "waiting to die." I knew I had to start writing, create courses, share my knowledge, and change this on a global level.

Everything you will read in this book will push you, challenge you, get you to dig deep, and inspire you. I've included a roadmap, some tools for kicking ass in the second half of your life, and lots of tips and stories to read. I will give you thought exercises and action steps along the way. These will require you to put down the book and pick up a pen and paper. Yes, you must write these down if you truly want to begin your kick-ass life, because simply thinking through these exercises and moving on won't fully prime your brain for the change they will help bring about.

Before you question whether you should stop to write down your answers to these thought exercises and action steps, know that writing them is super kick-ass important. Thinking about your answers doesn't prompt change because your answers remain in thought form and will pass right by you. When you write things down, you have to figure out the words and the why and take the time to make sense of those in a coherent way. We don't like unpleasant things, so our mind glosses over them. Writing requires a different part of your brain and slows things down.

To make things easier, I've included all of the thought exercises and action items in an appendix at the end of this book as a helpful reference, but don't turn there prematurely.

I promise that if you fully commit to this transformation, you will get new insight into discovering your vision and finding passion and purpose. You'll learn how to get your mind out of the dark places and finally figure out how to eliminate procrastination. I'll introduce you to ways to find more time. Initially, you will need to give yourself permission to spend time on things today that will give you more time tomorrow. Eventually, you'll start to have days that aren't filled up and your choices will start to be focused on kick-ass goals and a new way of living your life. It's awesome, let me tell you. Sharing the awesomeness I've discovered with others is the very reason I wrote this book.

You are amazing just the way you are, and you have a lot to offer. If you didn't, then none of this would matter, and nothing I've written in these pages would be of any consequence, because everyone over fifty or sixty could just spend the rest of their lives watching television until they passed. But you don't want that, and I don't want that for you either. The world deserves your best and everything you still have left in you. I found what works for me, and I believe it will help you too. I want everyone to discover their own best journey to their kick-ass second half of life.

Along the way, you will get as gritty as a cheese sandwich in a sandstorm. Will you have opinions? Does a bear shit in the woods? And do I care about your opinions? Nope...and neither should you. Move past those. What I *do* care about are the actions you take. These actions will shift you. If you are still reading this, then you are already starting to commit. This is great news!

You may be wondering how I came to discover the importance of the second half of life and making it count. This whole business of thinking about the second half of my life started when I was twenty-five. That's how old I was when my father died. We weren't close. He drank a lot, smoked a lot, hit a lot, and yelled a lot. He was racist and sexist, and when he was driving, everyone on the road was a "goddamn son of a bitch." You get the idea. I spent my teenage years leaving the dinner table early several times a week because I couldn't stand his racist talk. But, being the youngest, I grew up having to appease him and spend time with him because nobody else could or would.

When we went on the rare vacation, he would randomly pull over, stop the car, and go into a tavern to drink while we waited in the car...for hours. I was the one who had to go in and talk him into getting back in the car. I was a teenager! Self-absorbed and embarrassed. He was definitely not racking up the Good Dad points.

The one and only lesson I learned from him was to make sure I was not like him. As you can probably guess, he was not my favorite person. Yet these experiences started me on my path of self-discovery and a lifelong journey.

My mother took my father to the emergency room late one night for indigestion and chest pains, and the doctors decided to keep him overnight for observation. He died during the night of chronic obstructive pulmonary disease and other related health issues. Honestly, I wasn't sad. Well, I guess I was sad for my mother because she was feeling guilty that he died alone in the hospital.

But me? I was pissed! I was pissed at him for dying and pissed at myself for being such a self-righteous prick and not getting to know him any better. I had never asked him if he had any dreams or if he wanted to do anything more in life. Perhaps there were things he used to do, things that he really liked but didn't do anymore. I. Never. Asked.

Maybe it was all of the drinking and abuse at the time, but I never even thought to ask him those things until after he died. There was never an opening or invitation to have these types of conversations. I do know one thing for sure: he didn't know anything about me. He could not figure out why I would go to college when I could just get a job. I now call this "old-world mentality." The reality is that we were worlds apart in the way we saw life.

When I went to the hospital to pick up his things, I waited in the lobby while everyone rushed here and there, and I tried to ignore the crappy antiseptic smell hospitals seem to ooze. After several minutes, a woman brought me a brown paper grocery bag with my father's few belongings, and I got such a weird feeling. Here was my dad in this paper bag. This was it; this was all he had. I thought, "What a bloody waste of a life."

He never contributed anything I could remember except three daughters, and they didn't bring him any pleasure either. However, looking back now, I have often thanked him for waking me up to what life has to offer. I still do, because at that very time, in the cold, smelly hospital, right then and there, I made up my mind that when I got older, I would *not* waste my life. I would figure out what it took to do things and contribute, to be happy, to connect, to build a life of purpose, and to leave a legacy. I really had no clue what that actually meant, but I was determined, and determination was all I needed.

After that day, I truly cannot remember giving it much thought until I was sixty and on my early morning walk along the Deschutes River with my four dogs. While I was walking, a thought jolted me, like a flash of electricity. "What are you going to do about this life you have, Kathleen?" "I have no bloody idea" was my first reaction! It was right there that my journey started. Let me tell you, it has been the scariest, most thrilling, and most rewarding roller-coaster ride you could ever imagine.

Strap in, sit tight, get ready, and let's do this! You are here, and you have continued to read my story, so let's get to the "what the fuck" and do this!

Chapter 1

HOW THE HELL DID WE GET HERE?!

Let me start by saying this: obviously, you already stand out from the crowd or you wouldn't be here. You are different from most because you want to modify your current results. I appreciate that. You might not know this now, but the world will appreciate it too. In my opinion, we do the world a disservice if we do not live our best possible kick-ass life.

I have talked to many people over the years and I'm amazed at what I have learned about humans. Aren't we the best? I also did some research on all of the amazing things we have accomplished during our time here on Earth, and it would take a bunch of books just to list them, let alone tell the stories about the heroes who did the work. But I can tell you this: as humans, we have all of the resources, knowledge, and energy to create whatever we want on this planet. Most people, sadly, will never know this or do the work, even if they *do* want to unlock the kick-ass-life universe.

CHANGE YOUR WAY OF THINKING,
CHANGE YOUR LIFE!

The bottom line is this: humans are living longer lives than ever before and we need something to show for our time here on Earth! In the last few decades alone, we have entered a whole new way of aging that has never been done before. We cannot rest on our laurels. With everything we have discovered, continuing to live in that former space or mindset is such a waste of life.

CHANGING LIFE EXPECTANCIES

Let's back up a little bit and briefly explore life expectancy and aging, as well as how we got here. Thousands of years ago, when our ancestors were wandering around, exploring and evolving, they probably only lived for about twenty years. There wasn't much time to grow up, procreate, and take care of the kids or learn anything new. Then new tools and other developments gradually added to the number of years people lived, but it wasn't until the mid-1800s that life expectancy in parts of Europe and the United States crept up to the mid-thirties.

Life expectancy in the US climbed up to forty-seven years in 1900, then up to sixty-eight years in 1950, and in 2015, life expectancy in the US reached seventy-nine years. How did that happen? First of all, there was a major shift in how society looked at children.

Health officials and children's advocates started looking at what needed to be done so children could live longer and be healthy. In 1900, 25 percent of children died before they reached the age of five. Tragically, you can see evidence of this in any cemetery in America. Society began to look at how all those deaths had happened, and with the advent of new technology and medicine, the life expectancy changed, and more children lived to adulthood. Also, according to Laura Carstensen, director of the Stanford Center on Longevity, as that happened, the average birth rate for American women went from 4.2 to 2.1. That meant fewer children were being born.

Doctors and scientists discovered causes of diseases, and through health programs were able to inoculate children so they wouldn't have to endure symptoms that, in the past, would have shortened their lives. Supplements were put into food, milk was pasteurized, and food sources were available throughout the year. Government and health officials paid more attention to the water the public drank, and purification systems were used. Another boost to our lifespan came with garbage disposal and sanitation systems. Most of these things we take for granted now, but it wasn't always so.

In addition, after child labor laws were passed and a system of public education was developed, many more children learned how to read and write. With education came more opportunities and choices. This sounds wonderful, but the sobering fact is that a few years from now, there will be more people over the age of sixty than under the age of five, and four to five generations of people will be alive at the same time. We couldn't have imagined that would happen even twenty-five years ago.

Even though there is cause for celebration, there are also storm clouds on the horizon. Many people have begun to question whether the larger numbers of older people will drain resources or add to them. There is fear, apprehension, and some panic about what the hell to do with so many older people who have numerous medical, physical, and emotional needs. This actually presents a huge problem for many societies. There are too many of us, we are too sickly, and we have become a burden on the economy. We have too many problems; we aren't supposed to live this long. Well, let me say this: I am confident that we can turn this kind of thinking around, and in a short time, together. Here we are now, living a long time and moving toward living to at least one hundred. Millions of us. What matters is what we do about it, who we are while we're getting there, and what kind of guidelines we can set up for the waves of people following in our footsteps. Don't you think it is time to accept the responsibility for making sure the future is a place where everyone looks forward to exploring when they reach a certain age? We can do this!

Are you getting excited? Damn well better be, because this is a ride you want to take—with your arms up and yelling, "Wahoo!" Will it be scary? I'm positive it will be. It wouldn't be an adventure if it didn't scare the shit out of you, would it? The world doesn't need a bunch of wimps as guides. No siree, Bob! It needs experienced, skilled, fun, insightful, talented—did I say fun?— amazing people. That is and can be YOU! Well, me too, so I guess that means US. We are the ones. Don't you love the thought of it?

FACING BIG PROBLEMS

If I were sitting with you right now, I'm pretty sure you would admit that the world is facing some serious problems right now. On all levels and in all corners. We have the global warming problem, an energy shortage, the junk we have piled in our oceans, differing opinions on whether we should have affordable or free healthcare for all, how to ensure education for all (and that includes girls worldwide), pollution, homelessness, environmental destruction, total disregard for animals and plants, and it goes on and on. I hope you have your own list. We're going to need it. I told you that we were going to dig into some real shit here. This book isn't just about reading and doing; it is also about us all connecting, communicating, and leading change.

I've been talking with people around the world for a long time now (over fifteen years) while watching, listening, learning, and asking lots of questions. It is clear to me that for every problem out there, one or more people have the answer to solving it. It is a matter of getting people together and maximizing potential and outcome.

Have you stopped in on Google lately to check out how gamers problem-solve? I mean, not the weird ones, but the really smart ones. It is mind-blowing. More about that later. Now just think about that for a minute, and I think you will agree. There is a collective brilliance when a group of people have similar interests and ideas. And that is exactly what we are. A collective group of kick-ass-mindset individuals.

I understand there are many of us who feel lonely, not recognized, not needed, or even not wanted around very much. Many on this planet feel a loss of connection. All of that is about to change.

I had a friend who was lonely but always complained about everything and really drove people away. Myself included. This person felt that family and friends should always be calling and inviting him places and doing things for him just because he was older and was related to them or had known them for a long time. But that isn't how life works. As you will learn in later chapters, our attitudes, mindset, and motivation, along with how we take care of ourselves and others, are the pillars of who we are and what we can accomplish. Sitting around feeling entitled just because we have reached a certain age is horse pucky.

PLOTTING OUR COURSE OF ACTION

Let's revisit the "second half of our life" people again here. Us. In a few short years, we will make up over 20 percent of the population. One out of five. There will be lots of us out there, and it is up to us to figure out a way to keep connected and active, creating change and knocking the crap out of the myths of how we are supposed to be as we get older. Right now, only 1 percent of the world's population is over one hundred years old. Well, times will be changing, and we are going to be the change makers. By the time you get through this book and plan your course of action, you will have a roadmap for what lies ahead, and together, we can plot our course. Our path, our course together, is based on what we want and not some made-up idea of what we should be doing. To hell with that. Make sure you note how and where you can connect with me. I am on Facebook, email, and Instagram. (Okay, occasionally on Instagram, but I am still there and get my messages.)

I want to be clear: there is no blame here. Millions of people living over one hundred years hasn't happened before. Doctors, advertisers, designers of clothing and housing, nutrition experts, you name it, are basing their products, services, and attitudes on what they already know. We are going to challenge that by demanding what we want and need, and we are not going to be shuffled to the back room next to the brooms and mops. Nope. We are going to be in the front window, out on the sidewalk, at the front entrance. We owe it to the people following in our footsteps to create a future that celebrates being older and helps everyone to realize their potential.

As much as I like being an introvert, I decided that being visible is really important to making our presence known. If we are going to be one out of every five people, then we need to be seen. I also knew this had to start with me. I certainly couldn't ask other people to step up if I wasn't willing to do so myself. So I went to some Pride parades, joined groups to learn more, read articles, listened to people I respect, and attended some demonstrations and rallies for issues that are important to me. No, I wasn't on the front line waving a banner, but next time I might be.

I also write reviews of things I buy, places I go, and services I get. Here is the main thing I think is important: even if the service is shitty or the product is a piece of crap, in the review, I say what would make it better. I share what didn't work and why that affected my decision. Just demeaning someone or calling them names or disrespecting them isn't who I want to be. Education is key to getting what you want and need. Try it and see the reaction you get.

When you see or hear something that isn't okay, then say something. Remain calm but direct and purposeful. When I was doing mediation and conflict resolution, we had a workshop on interrupting racism. I learned a lot and used this knowledge a lot, but I have expanded my interruptions to all microaggressions I see and hear, whether they are racist, sexist, homophobic or transphobic, ethnic, ageist, or any other way humans show disrespect toward each other. Let me tell you, people get wide-eyed and quiet when I start in on them. But once again, it is an educational opportunity. First of all, it is important to stop what is going on. Say, "Hold on" or "What did you say?" or "Excuse me!" Then stick to what you are feeling. You could say, "I'm really uncomfortable with what you said" or "What do you mean by that?" Always give people a chance to explain and then follow up with how it is wrong and hurtful. We have a lot of power, and using it in a way that can create dialogue or make someone think about what they are doing can move you to the head of the line.

As a group (the over sixty years of age group) we have the power, knowledge, know-how, and reasons to get what we want, when we want it, and how we want it. We have a shitload of buying power too. Not for what there is now, but for what we will be needing and wanting on our journey.

ARE YOU "DECREPIT" OR UPGRADED?

Check this out: here are a few of the words listed when I googled "words for aging." Are you ready for these?

Crinkly.

Old hat.

Gumboot.

Old folk.

Old-timer.

Doting.

Decrepit.

Doddering.

Tottery.

This list brings me to my first ask of you. Ready? No? Okay, do it anyway. Push yourself. After reading my instructions, put this book down.

THOUGHT EXERCISE / ACTION STEP

Make a list of all of the words you have been called, heard other people called, or heaven forbid, you have called people you think are "old." Include words that you have called yourself in this list. You know, those times when you put yourself down, whether it was out loud or as that lovely inner voice that constantly shows up.

Now, let me ask you this: is "old" how you see yourself? What if you turn that around? Maybe instead you see yourself continually upgrading each year. Yes, I just said upgrading. If we got younger, it would be a downgrade, right? That's one of the reasons I love positive thinking. I have turned this "old" voice around, and instead I refer to myself as upgrading every year. Lesson number one: start to work on your voice now because *you are not old!*

There is no way in hell someone who is thirty or forty or whatever can possibly know what it is like to be seventy-five or eighty-five or even sixty. They think they know what it will be like, but that belief is based on how older people are often portrayed in the media. They are scared shitless of what they think they know, but the truth is that they are frickin' clueless. I realize this is a rant, but I am sharing this because changing the way we live our lives in the second half can change the story for them too. You know, the humans who haven't upgraded to our level yet.

Oh, and I love this one (insert sarcasm emoticon here): "I know how you feel." Bullshit. You are forty-four and you have not lived my life. Don't say that! Why not just say, "Wow, that must feel (insert the word that applies here: terrible, scary, bad, etc.)"? No one can know how you feel. They can empathize with you and hold your hand and give you a pat on the back, but know how you feel? No way. "That must feel scary!" Now that is something everyone can relate to because everyone has been scared at one point in their lives.

LIVING OVER ONE HUNDRED

Okay, let's talk about blue zones. Right now, there are five places in the world where people regularly live to be over one hundred years old. Soon it will be common for people worldwide to live to be one hundred. These five places are called the blue zones. A ton of studies have been done on people who live in these areas, as if they are animals in a zoo, and most of the information researchers have found is what you would expect from rather quiet and isolated communities with similar needs. What is so fascinating is that these people have the same resources as people in other places, but the difference I see is determination (there is that word again), taking action, and a healthy mindset, which of course lowers stress. People who have lived long lives in blue zones have some super-interesting tips. I have a blog post about this on my website, www.kathleensinclair.com; just search the term "blue zones" to check it out.

Where do you live? Inner city, farm, house, apartment? Do you live by yourself or with others? Are you still working? Are you in good health or bad health? Most of us are not able to live in the blue zones or choose not to, and although I love the blue zone tips and way of life, there are things that they do that I do not. I'm telling you here and now, though, I will definitely live to be over one hundred. I'm certain of it.

> ### THOUGHT EXERCISE / ACTION STEP
>
> Here's an interesting little side exercise for you: take a moment to pause and write down how long will you live. And by live, I mean be healthy, have a sound mind, and be able to contribute to society. Take that number and put it away somewhere with the date on it. You can and will look at it later on.

I wrote down 120. I said, "I want to be holy-shit old." What can I say? That's what came to me, and for once, I didn't set up the debate team in my head and battle it out.

THE SILVER FEAR

Let's dig even deeper into the facts here and move on to chat about the Silver Tsunami. Since economic growth has slowed somewhat for a few years now, many officials have tried to figure it out, and they came up with their great theory that there are too many old people. They decided to name it to give it a fear factor. The Silver Tsunami. The pyramid shape of the population has started squishing down with so many older people floating to the top, and now the damn thing looks like a rectangle. Woe is me. How can there possibly be enough young people to support all of these old fogies hogging all the money and resources? Now, this isn't just limited to the US. Nope, this fear is whipping through like a wind from the Sahara. The leaders of the G20 nations have even put aging on their priority list for discussion when they meet.

According to the Stanford Center on Longevity, these demographic changes have never been seen before. In Japan, the life expectancy in 1950 was sixty years, and now it is eighty-four. The number of centenarians (people who live over a century) is now the fastest-growing demographic group. Numbers like this are also seen in lower-resourced countries like Ghana and Niger. In 1950, life expectancy in Ghana was forty-one years and is now sixty-three years, while in Niger it was thirty-four years in 1950 and is now sixty-two years. But the problem in those countries is that childhood deaths remain very common. In Malawi, the number of people over sixty is expected to go from 4.1 percent of the population in 2020 (784,300 people) to 7.3 percent in 2050 (2,784,000 people). These developing areas account for 68 percent of the world's population over sixty.

A UN Department of Economics and Social Affairs report, *Inequality Matters*, brought up the idea that the developed world got rich before it got old, but less-developed regions will get old before they ever get rich. This just magnifies the fact that aging is a challenging global issue. Our role as kick-ass change makers and explorers is more important than ever, as we can set an example about aging that hasn't been experienced yet. Right now, the world is not prepared for the near doubling of life expectancy. It has happened so fast that social infrastructure, societal norms, and individuals' life plans are not ready. Waves of uncertainty and doom are blazing through government policies and infrastructure that looked vastly different from the current assumptions about the numbers of old versus young.

Think of the current norms in work, education, healthcare, and financial security. Think of the definitions of family, politics, and insurance predictions, as well as Social Security. Yikes. Think of traditional policies around education, length of working careers, health policies, and financial sustainability of pensions.

There have to be major revisions. Retiring in your sixties is not going allow you to support yourself into your nineties unless there are dramatic shifts in policy.

That isn't all the grimness that is festering. Haven't we had enough of this already? Evidently not. Some economists and politicians are predicting a major decline in productivity and an increase in strains on healthcare, making costs such as delivering care, wages, equipment, supplies, land, and buildings increase even more. Some feel there will be so many older people that their needs cannot be met with the current projected resources. Others feel that young and old will be vying for the same resources and that children and younger people will be left in the dust as older people consume too much.

Maybe developing countries can learn from the mistakes leaders in some developed countries are making now and plan better for their aging societies. Let's hope the policymakers take note and plan well for the future. At seventy-six, when I am writing this, I can feel the pressure and some buildup of anxiety about getting older, but I have to say, with our skills and experience, finding a new purpose is one of the most amazing opportunities for people over sixty.

I am not an economist, but I know that the costs of an aging society are churning up dread and panic among many people in power. Sort of like standing naked on an island with no shelter and watching the hurricane approach. Well, okay, there is one tree. Anyhow, I digress.

Warning: I am going to get all quotey and resource-focused here for the next few pages, but you have to understand the numbers and facts so that you know how to drive change within yourself and on this the planet. Okay, here goes. The *New York Times* economics writer Eduardo Porter pointed out that "the aging of the American population is carving an unexpectedly broad path of destruction across the economy... Many of our most intractable economic ills can be traced to some degree to this ineluctable fact: America is getting old." (I had to look up "ineluctable," and I am still not sure how to pronounce it.) But guess what, fearful leaders? Workers in the second half of their lives are working longer. Economist Andrew Scott at the London School of Business calculates that 90 percent of the increase in employment in the US has come from workers fifty-five and older. People in the labor participation force aged sixty-five to sixty-nine increased from about 28 percent in 1998 to 38 percent in 2019 for men, and for women it rose from 18 percent to about 30 percent. Also, according to the Kauffmann Foundation, the proportion of new entrepreneurs who were between the ages of 55 and 64 increased from 19 percent in 2007 to 26 percent in 2017.

We are productive workers with a shitload of experience. And according to Joseph L. Coughlin, in his book *The Longevity Economy: Unlocking the World's Fastest-Growing, Most Misunderstood Market*, "Thanks to their ingenuity and economic demand, the boomers have the potential to open up possibilities for older adults across the economic spectrum, across nations, and even far into the future." Now, that's more like it. And from the publication *Silver to Gold: The Business of Aging* by Paul Irving and co-authors from the Milken Institute's Center for the Future of Aging, "Older people stand out for their combination of experience, interest, and ability to fill skill gaps. They are a human capital resource that is ready to contribute to companies, younger colleagues, and a vibrant economic future." But American society, employers, and others who could benefit are slow to recognize what is in front of them. And we know that ageism and age discrimination are still active and doing damage. (Spoiler alert: you will read about Maggie Kuhn, the founder of the Gray Panthers, who challenged that and got laws changed, in Chapter 7.)

Economist Tyler Cowen from George Mason University says, "I would suggest that the ability to spot, mobilize and deploy older workers is the next biggest source of competitive advantage in the US companies. The sober reality is that many companies should retool their methods to fit better with the experience and sound judgment found so often in older workers." But you know what? This isn't the fault of employers or policymakers. It is no one's fault, really, because older people are supposed to be invisible and fade away, so who is going to even notice unless we figure out a way to conk them on the head with greatness?

Another person who has written extensively on the aging issue is Marc Freedman, who wrote the very informative and helpful book *Encore: Finding Work That Matters in the Second Half of Life*. He talks about reinventing the whole concept of retirement for the baby boomers, who are going to be living many more productive years.

Later on in the book, I will talk about Marc's work and what is possible for us. As it stands now, he sees the economic and social problems that threaten the world due to large numbers of older people leaving the workforce and expecting the smaller number of working age adults to pay for their expenses. Well, damn, this causes resentment, and it doesn't have to. Freedman proposes a different kind of retirement, with a phased-in transition from one career to a second career.

Sure, you can have the retirement of relaxation, travel, spending time with the kids and grandkids, and doing not much of anything, but when that gets routine, it is time to look at the possibility of a second, purpose-driven life using all of your experience and skills, and maybe even new training. And that seems like a wonderful way to live the second half of your life. This is a new way of thinking. Stay open to it because this is vital to living a kick-ass second half of your life.

There are other notables whom we will read about later on in the book, but right now I want to share something from my good ol' friend Bruce "the Boss" Springsteen, who said, "Aging is scary but fascinating" in his 2016 memoir, *Born to Run*. He also said, "Great talent morphs in strange and often enlightening ways." Well, who would know better than Springsteen, who reinvented himself at age sixty-eight and began telling stories about his life to packed houses at the Walter Kerr Theater in New York?

THINKING ABOUT RETIREMENT DIFFERENTLY

You probably know someone who—or maybe even you, yourself—could be added to the list of people who are confused with what retirement is supposed to look like. These people didn't look in the mirror and say, "Well, now that I am retired, I'd better hang it up." Nope. More than likely, they fully intended or still intend to remain vital and relevant and living their purpose. We know about lots of people who continued on in life to accomplish amazing and wonderful jaw-dropping things, but what we don't know or often see is how hard it was for them to get there. Reinvention isn't easy, and it has to happen in all aspects of our lives: from how we live day to day, interact with other people, manage our time, and handle our health, among other things.

Surveys have been telling us for a long time that the happiest people are those over fifty-five. Laura Carstensen, director of the Stanford Center on Longevity, says that this is this age at which people are the most positive and enjoy the greatest day-to-day satisfaction. Damn straight, Laura! Carstensen says there is a paradox of aging where the older we get, the happier we are, which, for many people, is the result of having more money and fewer bills to pay. At the same time, individuals recognize that as they age, they still have much to give and have the energy and desire to stay in the game.

One of my favorite quotes is from Chip Conley, founder of Modern Elder Academy and author of *Wisdom @ Work: The Making of a Modern Elder*. Conley says, "The first half of our life is about being interesting. The second half is about being interested." Mic drop. Well said. Truly, I couldn't have said it better myself.

We need to recognize that it is a whole new, fast-paced world out there, and we will need to adapt. Maybe it is a job loss, a partner dying, a parent needing care, or a change in health that jolts you into thinking about your priorities in the second half of life. This isn't about just staying alive and slogging on. It is more about making this second half a relaunch, a reinvention, a reboot into a life that has purpose and meaning and makes us smile. You want to wake up and welcome each day. Don't you? I'm assuming that your answer is yes, because you just read this sentence, and you are still here. Excellent! Read on…

START THE JOURNEY

The best way to get to this kick-ass zone is to start with yourself. Realize that this won't happen overnight. You are on a journey, and this takes a lot of self-reflection, from your health to your relationships to your financial security. This means figuring out what you want the next thirty, forty, or fifty-plus years to look like. Maybe this starts with getting off the couch and switching a sedentary lifestyle to an active one. Part of reinvention is figuring out a way to drop bad habits and adopt better ones. The Yoga Alliance reports that 14 million people over fifty-five have taken up yoga, up from 4 million in 2012. There are also huge increases among this group in hiking, canoeing, and cycling. And I am one of them.

I've always hiked, but when I lived in Mexico, I was a member of the kayak club and went out several times a week on Lake Chapala. I even bought an electric bike on a fundraising platform so I could go anywhere and not be bothered by long, steep hills. Pshaw to those. Listen, if I can do these things, you can do them even better. It is dawning on people that even if they haven't been active before, they have time to do some fun things now and get healthy. And there are so many free videos of how to get started, figure out what you like to do, and then learn more. Have you ever heard this joke? What fits your busy schedule better: exercising one hour a day or being dead twenty-four hours a day? Lack of resources and energy is not an excuse. Actually, I can't think of anything that would pass as a valid excuse. The important thing is to do what YOU want to do this time, and not what your neighbors, your partner, or anyone else is doing. If you haven't been active, then start out slowly and get some confidence. Your body will appreciate it.

Never in human history have there been more old people than young, so now is the time to stay healthy and active and not be a burden. By now, we know that the pyramid depicting the old on top and the young on the bottom has flattened to a maple bar (without the delicious maple icing), but in some parts of the world, the population is looking like an inverted pyramid, leading to difficulty for those societies.

HOW MY JOURNEY STARTED

Here's the deal: gray is in and it is beautiful, so let's look at some of these opportunities and how to prepare ourselves for making growing older a game changer. You know it has to start with each of us individually. We do the work on ourselves so we are ready and able to take on the bigger challenges, which ultimately is our purpose on this planet. When I had that revelation about my dad and my own life, I felt I needed to start doing things. I wasn't sure what those things were, but I knew I had to do them. I bought books to start with, as they are my go-to for figuring things out.

After my divorce in my late fifties, this nice financial lady looked me in the eye and said I had to get out there and make some money. My daughters were still in middle school, and I was trying like hell not to disrupt their lives more than the divorce had done. I hadn't been employed for a few years and wondered what I could do with my Bachelor of Arts (BA) in English.

Listen, don't laugh. When I first went to college, I was majoring in political science and wanted to work for the CIA (Central Intelligence Agency), until I woke up and realized what harm and shit they were doing and switched to reading books. I could deal with dead authors and stories a lot better than I could with terror and corruption, but now that I had to support my daughters and myself, the BA in English wasn't going to put a lot of food on the table.

I found out I could get a master's degree in education while teaching, so I jumped in and started a program at the University of North Carolina. But that was so I could get a job and didn't necessarily have anything to do with a passion or a purpose. Those words weren't in my vocabulary yet.

I was teaching school, and that had a lot of challenges, but then I thought maybe I needed to teach in another part of the world. Challenge myself. I took this intensive course through Cambridge called CELTA, a month-long hard-ass course determined to make or break you as an English language teacher overseas. But it was the best certificate you could have to guarantee a position.

By this time, I knew teaching was just part of my lifelong dream, and I did like to travel. However, after applying to several places, I found that educational institutions in other countries didn't want someone over sixty. Swell. Age discrimination glaring right at me. All this training and nowhere to go.

It was around this time that I was starting to realize something was missing, but it would still be several years and lots of wandering around in the desert before I figured out what I needed do. This might be where you are, or you may be someplace different. I wish I had known about all of the things in this book when I was starting out on this journey in my late fifties. I also know that we are presented with what needs to happen only when we are ready to accept it. Otherwise, it remains invisible to us.

It's obvious we have come a long way, and it's even more obvious the world needs what we have to offer more now than any other time in history. Now we understand our background and how we got to where we are at this moment in history. In the next chapter, we'll do some exercises to start improving ourselves and, by extension, what we have to offer the world.

YOUR KICK-ASS MANTRA

"I am grateful for all that is unfolding in my life and all that is yet to come."

Chapter 2

TIME TO AIR YOUR DIRTY LAUNDRY

Listen, I know you've done a tremendous amount of work in your life to get this far. No doubt about that. You could overflow rivers with the tears you've cried over your mistakes and fill a swimming pool with the money you wasted. You could start a new world with the time you've wasted. But none of that matters now. What matters is what you are going to do from this moment forward to create a new way of looking at the world (we are challenging aging here, so don't forget) through your smart, experienced, and insightful eyes.

This means we have to take off those old glasses and ways of looking at things and get down to what works NOW. First, we need to find out who we have become and see if we want to shift things around any. Get to know YOU, as in yourself. I'm still getting to know myself. It's a constant: we grow, we learn, we grow, we learn. This book is here for you and to focus on you.

Let's get started on some more action-taking work here. In this chapter, we're going to do some introspection, writing, and improvement. Are you ready for another list? Embrace it, and let's do this! This list is personal, and you will need a bit of time and space to get honest here. Writing things down makes that connection between your mind and your storage systems. I'll give you the prompts, and you will journal your answers.

DO YOU KEEP YOUR WORD?

I'm not talking about the namby-pamby stuff you say to others every day, but the things you say to yourself. Do you get up and exercise when you say you will? Do you call your relatives when you promise to call? Do you show up fully when you commit to things? Do you stop eating sugar when you promise yourself that you won't consume sugary foods anymore? Getting my drift here? If you are reading this, then chances are you already keep your word most of the time. Great!

THOUGHT EXERCISE / ACTION STEP

Examine whether or not you keep your word to yourself. Inevitably, there are times when you don't. Make three columns on a sheet of paper. In the first, write the situations where you don't keep your word. In the second, write down why you don't. In the third, write down what you will do to keep your word based on each newfound realization.

Be honest. Come on, no one is going to see this but you. You might find that some of the things you promise yourself really aren't that important and you can remove them from your self-promise list.

This action step is important for examination because before you can look outside of yourself and look at keeping your word to others, you must first be honest with yourself.

I still break my word to myself, but I have gotten a lot better after face-planting because of my stupidity a few times. A few years ago, I thought I was doing great by taking good care of myself and walking five miles a day, eating right, and doing all that other stuff you are supposed to do, but then I literally crashed and could not get out of bed. I had to call my daughter to drive forty minutes to let the dog out. I didn't get better for a week, although each day was an improvement. I thought it was a one-off and I would be up and running soon. Nope. I got flat-on-my-back sick for a week every month for two years. No diagnosis, no recommendations, no help. I would be fine and then drop like a brick. It took a while, but I finally figured out it was STRESS. Mental stress manifesting in a physical shit show of symptoms. I think I knew but couldn't figure out how to get out of it. Once I figured it out, the illness went away. A hurricane of reality hit me: I could not go through that again. I now know the symptoms like I know my favorite places to hike, and at the first sign, I take note and get the hell away from whatever is causing me stress.

Sometimes your stress might be caused by something as simple as not keeping your word about your time and what it means to you. Boy, I did that in spades when I volunteered for four hours a week at this great organization. Now, I know all the traditional guidelines about volunteering, such as going through a training program, committing to four hours a week for a minimum of six months, and helping out when other people are unable to show up for their time slot, as I have volunteered for a long time. I thought for sure I had it all figured out and had my guard up. Not a chance. One of my problems is that I love to help, especially when something is easy for me but seems so difficult for someone else. Anyway, four hours turned into twenty before I knew what was happening, and I had no one to point my teacher finger at except *moi*.

My first inclination was to make up some excuse and run for the hills and ghost them, but that isn't who I am either. So I had to suck it up, realize I had a spine in my back, and politely tell them, "I need to go back to my agreement of four hours a week. Where would you like me to work?" And you know what? They actually hired someone to do what I had been doing, so I didn't feel bad at all.

I used to lend my books and other things I had that people wanted to borrow. Even money. Gulp! I thought these people were my friends. I had to learn the hard way. It hardened me, too, which I don't like. Now I state up front what works for me and what doesn't regarding my time and things people want to borrow.

STOP IT WITH THE BLOODY COMPLAINING

Jeez. Nobody wants to hear it. Nobody gives a shit. Well, the negative blood- and energy-sucking people do, but you have to stop putting yourself in situations where you hang out with people who love complaining themselves and love listening to you complain as well. I'm not talking about problem solving and being a center of support for someone. I am referring to complaining about people, places, or things in life, in general. Got it? Just stop it.

I travel alone and live alone, and yep, I eat alone most of the time, so it is ripe territory when I am in a restaurant, tucked away at a small table for two, and multiple conversations are going on around me. Unless I am reading, I can't help but over-hear, and then I get the full wave of people's dumping. Holy crap! People like to dish the dirt when they get together. Not families so much, but groups, couples, and friends.

When I lived in Mexico, I lived in an active artist colony with a lot of Canadian and American expats and snowbirds. Around October/November, they would begin rolling in and the restaurants would fill up. They'd had six months of complaining to store up so they could dump on their friends and try to one-up each other with how bad things were for them, what tragic stuff had happened, and what terrible ordeals they'd had to endure. On and on. Yikes. It was worse than a shark-feeding frenzy.

They felt safe because the people getting the shit dumped on them were not present, they had a brand-new audience, and they were hungry for attention. What better way to lift your-self up while dragging someone else down, right? Ugh, this is so wrong. This kind of complaining will suck the life out of you, drain you, and hold you back.

I have a bunch of girl friends from high school. We still meet whenever a few of us are in the same place at the same time. And sure enough, some of them like to dish the dirt about people we knew over fifty years ago. Let it go, people. Give it up. Put that energy into designing your own life. Sheesh. I have, on more than one occasion, told them that what they were saying was absolute crap, untrue, and a complete waste of time. Complaining about people is a coward's way of getting attention. Don't do it. If your friends or coworkers are complaining, just pause the conversation, change the direction, and yes, tell them they are wasting their time and energy. Give some suggestions on new things that you could talk about and enjoy together.

I learned the following thought exercise / action step in a training program I did with Jack Canfield. It was a wake-up call for me and made me aware of how easy it is to fall into the complaining trap and the fact that it doesn't make anything better at all. I stopped being a reaction machine and took more time to think about what I wanted to say.

THOUGHT EXERCISE / ACTION STEP

Make four columns on a sheet of paper. In column one, mark down every time you complain about something for one week. In column two, list the date and time of those complaints. In column three, write what you complained about, and in column four, list your reason for complaining. No judgment here. Write down anything at all that falls into the category of complaining.

To get into the habit, you can start without the specifics by simply keeping a tally. Write it on the back of your hand, and at the end of each day, your eyes will be opened up when your entire arm is marked up with complaint tallying. It is way more powerful if you write down what you actually complain about, but right now, I just want you to become aware of how often you are doing this.

Some of my complaints were "I'm so tired; I didn't sleep well"; "Why can't I ever find anything, like the damn scissors?"; "Why didn't the stupid Amazon delivery guy leave the package where I said I wanted it?"; "Why does this always happen to me?"; and so on. The list was long.

Whatever you do, don't wait and try to remember the complaint later. How did that work out for you last time? Tally or write down the specifics as you find yourself complaining. An easy way is to go to the notes app on your phone and write one word that will remind you of what your complaint was about. That way, you won't run out of paper and your pen won't dry up. Or you won't complain about not knowing where your pen is. Then, have a look at what you wrote down. If you didn't write down anything, you are not being honest with yourself. This won't take you where you want to be in life. This is also called denial.

Next, take a few minutes to check out your tally or findings. Do you see a pattern? Do you complain at a certain time every day?

Do you complain about people—your kids, siblings, parents? Maybe about your aches and pains? What about politics or your house? What about the grocery store or lines or waiting on the telephone or the post office or... Can you see how this adds up? Complaining, in my opinion, is a relationship killer. Both with yourself and with others.

Once you write your list or tally, you need to step back, take a look at your complaints, and focus on how you are going to tighten things up a bit. What does that mean? What can you do to stop the complaining? Or, at the very least, to get into the habit of minimizing it? I like to replace my complaints with the opposite thought. For example, if you think, "I'm tired," replace this instead with "I am full of energy today—dang!" Or replace "I'm sick of being broke" with "I love how I attract money. All is well." Do you see how you just switch these around to the opposite thought? Even if you feel that the new thought isn't honest or it feels uncomfortable, still do it. One thing is for sure: by living in negativity and complaining, you are not being honest with yourself. Yes, it *will* feel uncomfortable. Do it anyways! If you get stuck, ask yourself, "How badly do I really want to change and live a kick-ass life?" This answer should always, *always* be "Really passionately! To my core! Badly!"

I am sure you have heard—at least once before—of keeping a gratitude journal. Consider this a reminder. I like to call it "my kick-ass thank-you book." According to an article on the online *Psychology Today* website, starting and keeping a gratitude journal can help you hold on to your relationships and boost your well-being. I don't know about you, but I need these kinds of things to help me thrive and move forward. If you don't want a paper journal, then download an app for this activity. The app that I use now requires only five minutes for me to say what I am grateful for, what I plan on getting done that day, and an affirmation. It is a way for me to focus at the start of the day.

This won't work if you think about it but don't do anything. If you keep on reading without at least buying a journal or downloading an app, then you will forget this suggestion in four, three, two...one. What were we talking about again? Oh yes, how self-help can turn into shelf-help if you let it. Most new things take about sixty days to become a habit. That thirty-day claim stinks like a stockyard. It takes thirty days just to find your groove and create a new neural pathway.

THOUGHT EXERCISE / ACTION STEP

Keep a gratitude journal. The best way to dive in is to start by thinking of one thing. What is one tiny little thing to be grateful for? Even if you think your life is a huge pile of the steaming brown icky stuff... what about breathing as an example of something for which you can be grateful? Try writing down one thing you are grateful for each day for one week. Then make a 100 percent jump and try writing down two things you are grateful for during the second week. And so on. You've got this. Do it.

STOP ASSUMING

Assumption is directly tied to fear.

If we can get the smoke to clear on this one, we will be taking a giant step forward to clarity, truth, understanding, better relationships, joy, and a whole new way of seeing the world. Would that be worth it? You bet your bippy. Question to ponder: why do we assume...well, mostly everything?! Furthermore, when we do make assumptions, why are they mostly negative? As kids, we learn all about assumptions at an early age. Unfortunately, we also do the Peter Pan thing and never grow up and shift out the assumption cycle. As an example, have you ever had someone in your life, whether your parent, sibling, friend, or neighbor, say they would do something for you, and then, after you got excited and became attached to the thought of them doing it, they just didn't do it? After this happens a few times, we start to enter victim mode and assume they don't love us, they are mad at us, or we aren't important enough. The list goes on. Here's a big one from childhood that often still exists in adulthood: you ask for something specific for your birthday and then you don't get it. Do you assume that the person you asked forgot about you or maybe that you are unlovable? Maybe you did something wrong or you don't deserve the gift? Then you come to find out they had to make an emergency trip out of town, and it had nothing to do with you. Sigh...

This happened to me when I was three years old, and here I am, still remembering it. I wanted a teddy bear for Christmas. Christmas came and went. No bear. And that is all I wanted. Then it was my birthday two weeks after Christmas. Surely my bear would come. That was still all I wanted, and I made this clear in my three-year-old "are you listening" voice. No bear. But then, at the end of the day, a package was delivered from my grandmother, who was traveling, and it was my BEAR. I still have the bear. I only found out as an adult that my parents had known that my grandmother was getting me a bear, so they didn't get one, but still, the feeling of not being loved or listened to lingered like skunk spray on a dog.

Divorce can throw children into some of the worst assumption cycles well into adulthood. If Mom and Dad got divorced, then we really screwed up and we must be bad, right? It's all our fault. Making a list of assumptions can be a daunting task, so instead I ask that you write down what you can do instead of assuming the worst.

THOUGHT EXERCISE / ACTION STEP

Write out the top five worst fears you have related to assumptions. For example, "My worst fear is that someone will figure out I am a fraud or assume I don't know what I am doing at this new job." After you write out five, write out a kick-ass turnaround for each: "I'm very talented and deserve this job!" Using this kind of kick-ass turnaround thinking will help you cancel out the assumption before it takes over. If you happen to remember any assumptions from your past, write those down too. Maybe you made an assumption about this book or you made an assumption about your partner. Whatever you remember, write it down. The more you explore, the higher you'll soar.

If you are honest, you will have to admit that most of your assumptions are a pile of shit. You made them all up. You really have no proof to back up any of them, but you talked yourself into believing them. You thought you were right. So how did that go for you? How does it make you feel when you assume? You know the old saying, "To assume makes an ass out of u and me." If you want to make assumptions, then make big, bold ones that you have some control over. I assume that if I exercise five times a week for at least thirty minutes, I will feel better. I assume if I write five hundred words a day, my book will get finished. I assume that if I cook food I really like and it is fresh, it will taste good. Assume the hell out of that kind of thing. Just don't make stuff up. And if you do, then at least admit it. Awareness is powerful when it comes to personal growth. "That was a crock of crap and I made it up." Start *that* right now, okay? No, not tomorrow. Right now.

IS YOUR PLACE A FRICKIN' HELLHOLE?

The next bit of examining we need to do has to do with tidying up. No, not folding the laundry or sweeping the mat of hair off the bathroom floor. I mean cleaning up all of the shit-ass things you are doing or not doing so that you can create some thinking and reflecting space for yourself. We need new neural pathways for good habits and thinking patterns.

Let's have a look at what that could mean.

Cleaning out the garage. Hmm. When was the last time the car was in the garage? Have you used most of the stuff in your garage in the past two years? What about the past year? If not, and something isn't a tool that you like to have on hand, then donate it! Hey, I'm not judging here at all. I was a bad offender in the garage category. After divorce number two (that's all, folks!), I moved into a much smaller house with the kids, pets, and all of the accumulated crap from a larger house we had lived in when I was married.

I managed to get rid of a couple of storage units' worth of stuff, but I had boxes stacked top to bottom in the double garage with only small aisles in between. Maybe I looked for something a few times; I can't remember. Basically, we lived there for five years and so did those boxes. I could never use the garage. Not during snow, hurricanes, blistering heat, or anything in between. Nope. My car sat outside. When it was time to move, I sure as hell wasn't about to go through those boxes. That five-years-ago life was over and done with. I had a huge dumpster thingy brought in, and I put all of those boxes in there and never looked back. Okay, maybe I should have donated it all, but I wasn't in that thinking space. Donating and giving are good things. The real truth is that, at that time, I was pissed and angry about the divorce and having to raise the kids on my own, and frankly, I was in denial. Those boxes represented shit I didn't want to deal with, so they just sat there, weighing heavy on me every time I walked through the garage. They just had to go. I'm sure I threw away great stuff, but by that time, I didn't give a damn. That was the start of my journey to minimalism as well as the start of great healing. The journey took seventeen years. I don't have a garage now, but if and when I ever get one, it will be pristine and tidy and open for a vehicle. No boxes of unwanted emotions or regret.

Let's get back to you. Maybe your screen door is broken. Does the kitchen sink drip? What about the neighbor who lets his dog poop in your yard? Maybe you've never figured out how to work your damn smartphone. Hey, you have your list and I have mine. How much is it costing you to ignore or complain about it? Does it feel good when you ignore these things, or do they just weigh you down every single time you think about them? Imagine removing the weight from your thoughts. That's what needs to be done.

THOUGHT EXERCISE / ACTION STEP

Make a list of every single thing that you haven't fully dealt with in your home or office that keeps taking up brain space. These irritations and naggings won't go away unless you do something.

Write three columns on your sheet of paper. At the top of one, write, "Things that irritate me so much I want to kick something." At the top of the second one, write, "Delegate to." And at the top of the third one, write, "By when."

So, it might go like this: The screen door is broken. The screen is ripped, has holes, and flaps in the wind. Plus, mosquitoes and bugs are always getting into the house. Do you have the skills to fix it? Do you even want to fix it? Do you think after twenty years that maybe a new one is in order? Would you be willing to pay someone to fix it? Who might that be? Could you find someone on Thumbtack or another online service? Do you have a bunch of things that need fixing like the screen? Maybe you can brainstorm for five minutes to fix a problem that irritates you every time you go out that door. Write down some ideas in the second column. Then, in the third column, write down a date. And not next year. Make it soon. The next couple of weeks would be great, no more than thirty days.

Maybe you're thinking, "Well, if I knew how to fix these problems, I would have done it already." Hmmmm... Well, let me tell you this, excuses will drag you down every single damn day. To live a wonderful second half of your life, a certain amount of mental and physical purge is going to have to happen.

If you don't know how to fix the sink or the broken door, and so on...then here is a dandy word you might want to put to use: DELEGATE! It's an action verb. The dictionary meaning is "to entrust to another person." Brilliant.

For each item on your list, be creative when thinking about what needs to be done and how it might happen. Ask people if they know of someone who does this thing or look up how to do it on YouTube. If you don't have money, then trade services: walk someone's dog, babysit their kid for a couple of hours, or run an errand for them. You are one brilliant, creative machine, so get to it. No excuses. Excuses get rid of muses, meaning they get rid of creativity. You are going to need that clear, uncluttered space in your mind for what you really need to be doing. Remember, I mentioned the NEW neural pathways. It is time.

DO YOU FEEL THE NEED FOR
APPROVAL?

Don't take things personally. Even if we think we don't care
what other people think, we really do. I find that I am curious
about what negative things people say, but I don't change my
behavior because of these things, nor do they influence me. But
I am curious. Now look at this: you could probably think of a few
people you know who care so much about what other people
think of them that they are basically chameleons who switch
how they speak and what they say based on what they think the
other person wants. They don't have a single thought of their
own. Do you trust those people?

If you watch certain TV news shows or listen to certain people
on talk radio, then you are often being influenced by people
who want you to stop thinking for yourself and just become
part of the herd. They want you to nod your head up and down
and agree with everything they say. No original thoughts
allowed. These people get you to believe that you have to trust
what they say or else there is something wrong with you. Are
you with me here? Do you know what I am talking about? Are
you one of the herd? What other people think and say about
you is their business. It is none of your business, so don't even
listen. I repeat: *it isn't any of your business.* They are entitled
to their thoughts. They cannot hurt your feelings if what they
are saying is a pile of shit. Got it? If you don't believe the crap
they say and don't let it in, then you don't give it power. If I
told you that your hair is blue, but really it is brown, would
you say, "Why yes, it is blue. I didn't realize that"? No way! You
know that your hair is brown, so my opinion means nothing;
it's a bunch of crap.

I know you were probably taught to be a nice person and not criticize. If you can't say something nice, then don't say anything at all. I am wearing my hip boots for that one because it is a rolling river of crap. Say what you have to say. Be honest—mostly with yourself—and then stand tall.

THOUGHT EXERCISE / ACTION STEP

Think about things people have said to you in the past. If someone says something that niggles a tiny bit, like a mosquito buzzing your ear at 3:00 a.m., then for sweet baby Jesus's sake, do something about it. Look at it. Is what they said true? Is what they've brought up something that you love about yourself, or do you know it could use some tweaking? Does this fall into cleaning up some stuff? If yes, then do it. If not, then ignore it. Their business. Thank you very much.

DO YOUR BEST. ALWAYS.

How are we doing on this one? Here I am at seventy-six, so you might think I have this one down. Nope. Still working on it. However, now it has my attention. Again, maintain awareness, all of the time. Doing my best is something I look at every morning on my list of how I want my day to go. And I look at it again in the evening while I am writing up my list of things to do for the next day. Sometimes your best is just getting out of bed and standing at the window. I get it. Go with it and don't criticize yourself. But don't lie to yourself. If it isn't your best, then get to the bottom of it. Are you worried about money, frustrated with the spouse, or unsure of where to start on building a new bathroom? We're human. Whatever it is, write it out. Talk to someone. Talk to yourself. See if you can get help. Admit you are in a slump. Send a letter to Santa Claus.

If the stuff around your house and the tidying up has to do with grief, then go easy here. This can be like dropping something down a deep hole and never hearing it hit bottom. I heard a piece on *This American Life* about a Japanese man who had so much grief after his family was wiped out in the tsunami of March 2011 that he placed an old telephone booth and (unconnected) rotary telephone out in his garden. He called it "the Wind Telephone," as his calls to his missing and presumed dead family would go out over the wind. He talked to them all the time. Word got out, and thousands of people over the years have come to the garden to talk to their loved ones. My point is, if grief is the reason you are stuck in this area, maybe build a shrine in your home. A photo, a candle, a poem, a personal item. Put a wind phone in the garden of your mind and talk.

When it comes to everyday tidying, chores and routine actions often become mundane. Our minds frequently drift on autopilot. Cleaning up after a meal, taking out the garbage, doing the laundry. Done them thousands of times. Throughout this book, take time to think about the everyday things that you do on autopilot.

THOUGHT EXERCISE / ACTION STEP

Think about things you do in your life. Ask yourself, "Is there a better way to do this? Is there a tiny bit more I could do each time to make it easier for myself or for someone else?" Ask yourself questions; get curious with yourself. Getting curious with yourself means that you are always, always doing your best. If we train ourselves to do our best with things that aren't important to us, like everyday tasks, we will be setting ourselves up for doing our best all the time. That in itself will become a habit.

GIVE UP BEING RIGHT

Thinking back, I remember wanting to be right when I was quite young, maybe six or seven. Life wasn't too stable, dealing with a father who drank a lot and often didn't have work, living in post–World War II government housing, and trying to stay hidden from the yelling and hitting. The things I wanted to be right about was kid stuff, like throwing the ball farther, running faster, reading better. I'd be indignant, hands on hips and yelling at the other person. Of course, they'd be doing the same to me. But damn, it felt good when I would turn and walk away. It felt good. Evidently, it didn't matter if my claims were true or not because no one ever asked for proof, but it was that momentary "I'm better than you" feeling that made all the difference.

Somewhere along the line, I realized that the truth is the truth, and I don't have to defend that. Now someone can yell in my face all they want that global warming doesn't exist, and I don't give a rat's ass who they are or what they call evidence. The truth is the truth.

This often hits very close to home, and that is where this being right stuff can get sticky and messy, like an ice cream cone in a sandstorm. In listening to people who always want to be right, it seems they are often in the clutches of insecurity. They cling to their position in spite of mountains of evidence that they are wrong. This is certainly human. We need to feel secure and confident just to get through the day. And if there is someone we admire and look up to who is also wrong, then damn, it is our job to make that person right. We're seeing this in politics and other areas all the time. But look at the cost of these actions and beliefs. If you are determined to be right, then someone has to be wrong. And that leads to us and them, my tribe and your tribe, the smart ones and those other guys. Sound familiar?

I talk with many older people who say lots of negative things about younger people, and group all of them together as if they are the same. "Those millennials are so entitled." "Young people are lazy and don't know the meaning of hard work." When I talk with these older people, I often find that they feel no one listens to them anymore. They aren't of value anymore and they feel left out much of the time, particularly with their family.

If you are someone who feels you need to let people know you are right, try a different approach. Here comes that word again: be *curious* about what the other person is saying. Be a listener. If you need to, tell them that although you always felt your answer was correct regarding a particular situation, you are going to listen to what they have to say and be open to a new perspective.

THOUGHT EXERCISE / ACTION STEP

Whenever you are with a person who has to be right, but who you know is dead wrong, ask yourself a few questions:

1. Will anyone be hurt by this opinion?

2. Does it make any difference in the scheme of life?

3. Do I really give a damn if this person thinks they are right?

4. Am I willing to let it go, knowing that the truth of the matter is what counts?

Then hum a few lines of "Let It Go" and stop talking.

While you have been on this path, I'm pretty sure you have been faced with a lot of dragons, and not many of them have been friendly. Some you had to go over, some around, and some you just had to blast the shit out of and plow through. The best thing is that you are not alone. I've been there, and a ton more people on this globe have been and are there as well.

More great news: we have everything that we need to accomplish any task we choose in life. Maybe you won't be a Navy SEAL, but you sure can train like one. Speaking of training, in the next chapter, we're going to begin training our bodies, minds, and souls to prepare for our kick-ass lives. Let's learn how to be the best possible version of ourselves.

YOUR KICK-ASS MANTRA

"I am fulfilled. I am fearless."

Chapter 3

KICK-ASS VISION TAKES GUTS AND PURPOSE

Now that you are in the second half of your life, what is your purpose? Whoa, that's a big question. Okay, let me back up a little bit. Maybe you've spent many years working to support yourself, your family, and those you care about. I'm sure that you know your sacrifices helped many people have better lives.

Perhaps those people have now found their own way and are living their dreams. Now, what about yours? This is your encore. It is time to see where you want to be and how to get there, and then live that beautiful vision. Okay, Kathleen, sure, but what the hell does that even mean? Encore?

When we were young, we believed we could be anything and do anything. We could fly to other worlds and fight dinosaurs. We could become firemen or ballerinas. We could be basketball players or ice skaters. Our minds ran away with all of the possibilities, and we probably spent hours fantasizing about our future lives. But then reality, school, and lots of people telling you what to do changed all of that. It's called domestication.

You are what I like to call a second-half encore virgin. You bought this book because you wanted to find out how to live a kick-ass second half of your life. This means you can't keep doing things exactly the same way you have been. Okay, maybe some things, but probably not all. So, encore virgin, what are you going to do about this? What's your vision for all these wonderful years to come? One way to start defining this in order to get to an answer or set of answers is to look at your life and see how it falls into several categories.

At the end of this chapter, you're going to complete the thought exercise / action step of defining and mapping the first part of your vision. After you have read the following sections in this chapter, you can start defining your vision by diving into these main categories: health and fitness, which includes food and drink; family; parenting; love life; intellectual interests; and spirituality and religion. Of course, you can always add new categories to suit your own personal needs.

This is sort of "Life 101," and I'm here not to hold your hand but instead to poke you with what's possible to wake up and realize how much you deserve and have to offer. Your vision will help you achieve your best kick-ass life. Now is the time the world needs you the most, in case you hadn't noticed.

In each of the following six categories (health and fitness, family, parenting, love life, intellectual interests, and spiritual and religious) I recommend answering the following four questions. These are detailed more at the end of the chapter, where you do the Mapping Your Vision exercise.

1. What's true for me right now in this category?

2. What is my ideal vision in this category?

3. What are the reasons I want to achieve my ideal vision?

4. How the hell am I going to get there?

I am going to give you examples of what I wrote for two of the six categories to give you an idea of the type of ideas you can explore. But because this is highly personal, I will not fill out the others.

HEALTH AND FITNESS, INCLUDING FOOD AND DRINK

"Keeping your body healthy

Is an expression of gratitude to the whole cosmos—

The trees, the clouds, everything."

—THICH NHAT HANH

1. What's true for me right now?

I walk every day. I would like to be more flexible and stronger in my upper body. I don't go on long hikes right now and would like to get back to those when the weather is cooler. I eat a lot of organic veggies and hormone-free chicken and fish. I rarely eat beef anymore. I do qigong five times a week, along with stretching and squats. I drink lots of water but could probably drink more. I eat too many sweets and too many carbs.

2. What is my ideal vision in this category?

In my ideal vision, I see myself being strong, flexible, and having the endurance for a six- to eight-mile hike once a week.

My vision also shows me eating a more plant-based diet with less animal protein.

3. What are the reasons I want to achieve my ideal vision?

The reasons I want to live my ideal vision are longevity and being able to do the things I want to do. Living my purpose and continuing my mission for challenging aging.

4. How the hell am I going to get there?

I plan to realize my vision through my action plan, which is:

- Take daily three- to five-mile fast walks and mix up the routes because I get bored pretty easily doing the same thing over and over.

- Do strength training, carry weights, use bands.

- Use my body in resistance workouts and HIIT.

- Do yoga, tai chi, and qigong for flexibility and balance. Create twenty-minute routines for each of those, then switch them up.

- For food, eat a mostly plant-based diet with occasional pasta or rice. Eat free-range poultry and sustainably caught fish. Eat organic vegetables and fruits when available. Drink unbottled water and occasionally wine or other alcohol.

* * *

As a side note, remember to be good to yourself! Flexibility is the key here. For example, if I have time and I am not in a writing mood, then I do all of my exercises in the morning. However, if I need to write when I get up because the thoughts are flowing, then I intersperse the exercise during my breaks from writing and doing research. I will write for an hour and then do my qigong for twenty minutes, back to writing and then some work with the weights for ten minutes, and so on. Creativity and my "why" are important here; if I ignore them, I fall into the procrastination well and keep dropping.

If exercise and fitness are new for you, I recommend starting with a few minutes a day and building up to something that is challenging but makes you feel good and energized. Your body will thank you. Everything will function better, and your sleep will be great too. Remember why you want to be fit and healthy. Give it a go.

As for food and drink, you would think that after seventy-six years I could say I have had my cake and eaten it too, but not so. And whereas I no longer subscribe to the "eat your dessert first" philosophy, I do still enjoy a yummy piece of chocolate cake now and then or a chocolate chip cookie with crisp edges.

However, now I tend to listen to my body more and use the Japanese *hara hachi bu* idea of eating until you are 80 percent full or, more intuitively, thinking "I'm no longer hungry" versus "I'm full."

According to Dan Buettner, who writes about the blue zones— where people routinely live to be over one hundred years old— that I mentioned in the last chapter, to be successful with *hara hachi bu*, it is important to eat slowly, to focus on eating and not doing anything else, such as emailing, reading, or watching TV, and to use small plates. Now, is that asking too much to be healthy and live your best life?

I love all of the new fresh and organic markets that have popped up more and more in neighborhoods. These are great resources for getting closer to what you eat.

In certain areas, these markets go on year-round, stocked with the different veggies and fruits available at that time. Every time I travel to a new place, I check out their markets and find great fresh food.

Sure, it takes a bit more time and maybe it even costs more, but that is something I am willing to take into account to be a healthier person as I march toward greatness and peak performance. The bottom line is to know yourself and your strengths and weaknesses. Just work the hell out of those strengths, and see if you can't take the weaknesses by the hand and turn them into strengths too.

Okay, do you have an idea of what you are going to write down for the four questions now? Mainly, you want to get an idea of where you are and where you want to be.

FAMILY

"The bond that links your true family is not one of blood, but of respect and joy in each other's life."

—Richard Bach

For this section, we are going to look at immediate family: parents, grandparents, children, siblings, their children and spouses, aunts, uncles, cousins, and in-laws. All of the other people you consider family will be covered in the next chapter.

1. What's true for me right now?

I have two daughters, one grandson, one son-in-law, one sister, some nieces and nephews, and cousins. Some I see a lot, and some I haven't seen in years.

2. What is my ideal vision in this category?

I see a relationship with my older daughter and son-in-law remaining as it currently is, where I see them once or twice a year for a month or so and animal- and house-sit when they go on vacation.

My vision is blurry with my other daughter, as we have not spoken for over six months. I do not get to see my grandson, but we communicate regularly via messages and phone calls, so I see that continuing as a means of support. I do feel circumstances will change and so will my vision.

I have to say that I want more quality time with my immediate family members. "Quality" being the operative word here. My vision is to have strong, open communication with family members and a safe space for people to say what they need to say and get their needs met within the family circle.

3. What are the reasons I want to achieve my ideal vision?

I value open and honest communication and time with my immediate family. I appreciate their support, love, understanding, acceptance of me just the way I am and our fun times together.

4. How the hell am I going to get there?

I really wished I had that magic wand for this one. After thinking about it, I decided that communication was the first step and that I would first reach out to various members through their favorite or most used means of talking with people. For some, that is email, for others it is a phone call, with a few using Facebook and others preferring Messenger or other messaging apps. Based on the outcome of those conversations, I will proceed with ways to get us together.

I am going to ask them what they think, what they want, and for any other input they might want to share. Then I will tell them what I propose for getting together for a few days once or twice a year and see what they think about that. I will plant the seeds and see if they grow.

* * *

Families are complicated, wouldn't you agree? And so many secrets, stuff that gets shoved under the rug of denial, and refusals to budge are woven in there too. On and on it goes. Wherever you are right now is fine. It doesn't matter because we are going to be creating something better that works for us.

If that means seeing some people more or less, then so be it. This is one area where you will change as your family changes. One of my sisters died last year, so the plans I had for seeing her changed, and now I plan on shifting that time to my niece, who spent many years caring for her mother. She lives further away, and it will take some planning on our part to see one another regularly. My grandson is transgender and is going through the process of transitioning. Talk about family drama. Wowzers.

Many of you are probably still caring for your parents, so you know how important it is to maintain your freedom while still providing loving care to an older parent. My mother was sick for many years, and even when well she was not a happy or positive person.

Not only was the glass not half full; most of the time there wasn't even a glass. It wasn't until after she died that I realized I had spent most of my life trying to make her happy. Did that work? No, but I kept trying anyway.

I recommend you do not do that because, as you know perfectly well, it ain't gonna happen. That reminds me of a quote attributed to Abraham Lincoln: "Most folks are about as happy as they make their minds up to be." My mother made up her mind not to be happy.

It will work out best for everyone concerned if you make a reasonable plan you can honor. And think really hard about asking an older relative to live with you, especially if they have been living alone for a while and are independent. I'm not saying not to do it—sometimes it is wonderful for all involved. However, I have heard many horror stories, and you probably have too, about times when it doesn't work out and everyone is walking on eggshells and miserable.

I recommend not doing anything out of guilt. Just don't go there at all. Not with any members of your family. All of that guilt crap comes from the past, and that is over and done with; we are starting right now. Figure out a way to do what you need to do with love, kindness, and compassion.

PARENTING

"While we try to teach our children all about life, our children teach us what life is all about."

—**John Updike**

Remember the four questions to ask yourself in this category are:

1. What's true for me right now in this category?

2. What is my ideal vision in this category?

3. What are the reasons I want to achieve my ideal vision?

4. How the hell am I going to get there?

I have made a few comments about when I feel I still play the parent role, but it isn't often enough to fill out this category for myself. You can make your own decision about it.

Normally, parenting is thought of as something we do with our children until they move out on their own. I have found that it continues on in a different way, and this is probably true for many of you. I adopted my daughters when I was in my early forties, and they are in their thirties now. The parenting has shifted to me only offering advice when I am asked for it directly. I tried the other way and immediately found out I should keep my mouth shut...and I agree. They have their own lives, and just because theirs are different from mine doesn't mean their lives are wrong or bad or anything else.

When my mother was sick for many years, I found I was parenting her too. Many of the people I have talked with also take care of grandchildren, some of them every day, some of them a few times a year or during the summers.

When you take care of someone on a routine basis, the joy of being a grandparent and handing them off at the end of the day can shift to déjà vu of when you were a parent.

With my grown children, I have developed communication lines and worked hard to keep them open and be there when the going gets tough, which seems to happen pretty often. I believe that my role as a parent is to act as a pointer in a possible direction or as one who asks difficult questions rather than providing answers. I choose to work on communication as an important part of keeping the parenting link connected because I can do that from anywhere via phone, Zoom, email, or texting.

I also have found it beneficial if I draw some boundaries around when I am available or when I will respond. There are often grumblings because I "never answer my phone or messages." I keep my phone on silent all the time because I want it to be a tool for me, and I want to respond when I am in a place where I can listen and not be distracted. This was a HUGE factor in me getting to live a kick-ass second half of my life. I communicate via technology on my time, not others'.

LOVE LIFE

"The greatest happiness of life is the conviction that we are loved; loved for ourselves, or rather, loved in spite of ourselves."

—Victor Hugo

If you fill this one out, remember the four questions:

1. What's true for me right now in this category?

2. What is my ideal vision in this category?

3. What are the reasons I want to achieve my ideal vision?

4. How the hell am I going to get there?

I have been single for over twenty years. I love being single. So I don't even fill out this section. I know many people who are single and also love it. However, I have friends who long for another relationship, for someone to share things with and who can be a partner as they get older, and that is fine too.

If you are single and looking for someone, get very clear about what that someone looks like and acts like. Are they kind, compassionate, funny, generous, and honest? Are they your friend? Are they helpful and considerate? Do they like to travel? Are they financially secure? Are they healthy? Write down everything you think is important in a partner, and don't settle for less.

This is something you need to be very specific on; also include deal-breakers.

I have a friend whose list was four pages long. She was able to bend on some of the list items, but her deal-breakers were no alcoholics, drug users, molesters, or physical or mental abusers. She manifested the man of her dreams and the two of them have been married ten years. The deal-breakers sound like no-brainers, but seriously, write them down because you will know the warning signs immediately if you are more aware of your absolute "no ways."

Another thing to ask yourself is if you want to get married and live together or if you prefer to stay single or maybe not even live together. I know of a couple who lived about fifty miles apart and wanted to be together but not live together. One of them has property and a house, so the other one built a small house on the property, and they live next door and work it out that way.

I just went on a trip with a couple who travel together and do many things together but choose not to live together. You will know what works for you at this time in your life. Define what works for you in your vision and kick-ass life.

On a side note, in doing research for this book, I was surprised to find out that the divorce rate for people over fifty has doubled since 1990, and for those over sixty-five, it has tripled. From that alone, it seems that many people are rethinking who they want to spend time with now that they are in the second half of life and have a different set of choices. Go for it, and remember to have fun and laugh a lot. Enjoy the small things and be true to yourself. Your new, wonderful self.

INTELLECTUAL INTERESTS

"Anyone who stops learning is old, whether at twenty or eighty. Anyone who keeps learning stays young. The greatest thing in life is to keep your mind young."

—HENRY FORD

The four questions to ask yourself are:

1. What's true for me right now in this category?

2. What is my ideal vision in this category?

3. What are the reasons I want to achieve my ideal vision?

4. How the hell am I going to get there?

So, what is learning, and what does it mean for us as we get older? Learning covers different ways of stimulating your brain. Are you a lifelong learner? Do you take classes, meet with discussion groups, belong to a book club, use the hell out of your library card (you do have one, don't you?)? What do you want to learn? Why? How do you go about this?

Dear people, remember that this is about what you want to be doing from this point on. We're not using the retrospectoscope for your life here. All we have is NOW, and as we move forward into each now, the old shit is gone.

What is your favorite idea about the future of your learning and stimulating your mind? I hang out in this area a lot. I am curious to the point of being nosy sometimes, and I never get bored. There is always something I am eager to find out about, whether regarding people, nature, a car accident I see on the freeway, or how to see the wind.

People over fifty are going back to school in droves. Some go to level up their skills for their current job or one they want to go into, others go to finish something they started, and some go because they want to learn something new in a non-stressful way compared to when they went to college. Learning can mean everything from making a new dish for dinner to watching a YouTube video on how to stop the toilet from running. It can even include wondering if those mushrooms you just picked are edible. We're learning all the time, even if it isn't in a specific learning situation.

What about mistakes? I make so many mistakes that I feel like I have this Greek chorus following me around, continually calling me out while sneering and wagging their fingers. But mistakes are all a part of learning, and even though I do not like them, I have learned to give them a place at the table.

Think about where you are with lifelong learning, what it means to you, and how you want to integrate it into your future. You will know what works best for you. And when you have those ideas, be sure to write them down.

Writing all of your ideas down helps you remember and is also a starting point for making changes and additions or subtractions later on. What are you curious about? Learn more; it will move mountains for your soul and kick-ass life.

SPIRITUALITY AND RELIGION

"All major religious traditions carry basically the same message: that is love, compassion and forgiveness. The important thing is they should be part of our daily lives."

—Dalai Lama XIV

Remember to start with the four questions:

1. What's true for me right now in this category?

2. What is my ideal vision in this category?

3. What are the reasons I want to achieve my ideal vision?

4. How the hell am I going to get there?

This area is so personal that it is difficult to pin down, because it is different for everyone. I will just talk about what it is for me and leave it up to you to sort out for your particular beliefs.

This is an area I have explored for most of my life. I first did so through a formal church, which was a guiding force for me in my young years of turbulence because the message was always that I was good and that God loved me. There was never any of the high-handed guilt that gets passed out in other religions.

However, at that time, I melded religion and spirituality into one, and I don't even think we used the word "spirituality" very much, as I remember. Over time, I came to define religion as a specific set of organized beliefs and practices that were shared by a group of people, and spirituality more as an individual way of looking at the world but not associated with a fixed set of rules and practices.

I stopped going to formal "church" when I was seventeen, as I no longer got answers to my questions but rather heard responses more along the lines of "That's just the way it is" or "That's just what we believe." Not good answers for me, even at that time, because they weren't answers at all, just another way of adults saying they hadn't thought about it and didn't really know.

In my twenties, I studied Zen, read a lot of Watts and Krishnamurti, and looked into various theories about psychology and mostly Eastern philosophy. I checked out existentialism too. I was exploring different ideas. I read the Bible as literature and also studied Hinduism and Islam, more in the historical and literary sense and not in the religious vein. I never went back to attending a formal church and had reservations about attending church when raising my daughters. I didn't feel it was okay just to drop them off somewhere and drive on, but I also felt like a hypocrite if and when I attended a service. I always wanted to raise my hand and say, "Excuse me. I don't think that is what it says in the Bible, and furthermore, I don't think it means what you are saying at all." But I didn't do that, as I was a guest, so who was I anyway? Hence, no attendance by me. I still read a lot and explore various philosophies, but it isn't important to me to belong to a specific church or be part of a certain religion.

I respect all religions, and if people want to believe a certain way, then they need to do that. I do not respect people who use their religion as permission to do whatever they want, especially committing violence of any kind, and throw out a few religious phrases as a means of justifying what they do. Those people are scary and don't make much sense. If you are part of an organized religion and it brings you great joy and fulfillment, then that is where you belong. What could be better than that?

Ask yourself what experience and relationship you want to have with your particular beliefs in the future. Do you want to travel to a holy place? Do you want to study a particular area or spend time with religious leaders? Do you want to build schools in Africa or set up medical stations in Paraguay? Do you want to live in a place that supports your beliefs and where there are other people like you who find meaning living and working together? Maybe you want to go on a pilgrimage or retreat or become more involved in volunteering and helping out with your religion. This is the time to explore what that means to you and how you can fit that into your life.

Remember all of the things you thought you would love to do over the years and figure out a way to incorporate them into your life moving forward. You deserve this. For those who choose a more spiritual path or want to explore what that means, the dictionary defines spirituality as "the quality of being concerned with the human spirit or soul as opposed to material or physical things." Well, that is one way of looking at it, but I bet you have a different way if you consider yourself spiritual.

For me, it was looking for my purpose and looking at the large picture of humanity and life, figuring out how to give back, and learning how to make the lives of people who will inherent the Earth from my generation better than they are now. Wow, that was a mouthful. You might think of the exploration of spirituality like climbing a mountain where everyone takes a different path to the top but all arrive at the same place. I have met many spiritual people, and many of them have combined very old spiritual customs from different belief systems into their modern world.

If you look at the global community and how people from all over interact with each other, it is no wonder that new practices and ways of being spiritual are emerging all the time. For some people, a daily spiritual practice is beneficial, and that might be what you want to explore further. Others find spending time in nature a spiritual experience.

If you are thinking about ways to become more spiritual, try meditation. This can be a guided meditation from a YouTube video or a walking meditation for a few minutes several times a week or even daily. If walking, do so with purpose and be conscious of clearing your mind in a safe area. If possible, integrate yoga, tai chi, or qigong into your life a few times a week and take short breathing exercise breaks throughout your day.

Another very helpful practice is keeping a gratitude journal, as mentioned in the last chapter. Super. Powerful. Stuff. You can journal in the morning or evening. Write down three to five things you are grateful for each day. The body loves gratitude and releases little endorphins of goodness, and who doesn't want those?

Maybe you want to read books about spirituality or find a spiritual community of people who support each other. Whatever path you choose, find a way that speaks to you and how you want to be in the future for this lovely second half of life. Great job thinking through all of those categories.

That was a lot to think about. Congratulate yourself on taking the time to reflect and make decisions about your future that will guarantee you are living your best life.

MAPPING YOUR VISION

Determining what you want for each of these categories isn't something you will do just one time. Things change, desires change, and interests change...constantly. Which means revisions will need to be made at least every six months. It is very important to focus not only on your life now, but also what you would like your life to be like in a year, three years, five years, and so on. There are many ways to go about looking at all of the areas of your life; I shared what I do, but I encourage you to find out what works for you and what categories are important to you.

You've been asking yourself some questions as you have been going through these categories. Just remember that these are the questions I use, as they trigger me to start thinking in a different way. I'm sure you will have your own, but feel free to use these to start.

1. Begin with what's true about yourself right now. Find out what your beliefs and assumptions are for each category. What is the concept and mental image you have of yourself in each area? Write out where you are currently at. This is very powerful. For example, I am a retired teacher. You might find yourself writing things like "I do the same thing every day," "I currently don't have many goals or passions," "My health is okay, but I don't exercise consistently," and so on.

2. Next, write out how you see yourself in your ideal way. I am a retired teacher coaching other educators around the world on how to connect with their students. I travel the globe often. I have made time every single day to move my body and it feels great. See where I'm going with this?

3. Write out the reasons behind what you want to do in each category. This step is super powerful. The reasons are often eye-opening!

4. Finally, how the hell are you going to get there? Writing this down on paper is a start, but you need to be willing and able to do the hard work. Which means finishing this writing assignment (or "step," if that sounds easier for you) and then starting to move toward your vision in each category.

This is an area where you should dream big. I mean so big that you feel a bit of nausea and, yes, even disbelief. Don't deal with what you think might happen. Pass those thoughts over. Instead, write what you really, really, to your core want to happen. Look at all of this as an ideal place where you want to be within the next year, three years, five years, and beyond, and then move out in time to refine it all. Then say to yourself or write next to each category, "I am soooooooo doing this now!" Change isn't going to happen unless you think it is a possibility and you actually—to your core—commit to it. Once you make a decision, it is done. There are no negotiations with yourself. Look up the definition for "decision." Actually, I will save you the time: a decision is a conclusion or resolution reached after consideration.

THOUGHT EXERCISE / ACTION STEP

Recall the four "mapping your vision" questions.

1. Start with what's true about yourself right now. Find out what your beliefs and assumptions are for each category. What is the concept and mental image you have of yourself in each area? Write out where you are currently at.

2. Next, write out how you see yourself in your ideal way.

3. Write out the reasons behind what you want to do in each category.

4. Finally, how the hell are you going to get there?

Use those four questions to define and map your vision in each of these main categories:

- Health and fitness, including food and drink

- Family

- Parenting

- Love life

- Intellectual interests

- Spiritual and religious interests

Add your own categories if you feel any additional categories are needed.

Now that we've mapped our vision for the most important personal aspects of our lives, let's keep up the momentum and see what that vision looks like on steroids!

YOUR KICK-ASS MANTRA

"Forward progress, just keep moving!"

Chapter 4

YOUR KICK-ASS VISION ON STEROIDS!

This chapter includes the categories where we spend much of our time with people other than our families. And many people spend most of their time with those who are not their traditional family members. As in the previous chapter, the thought exercise / action steps for the categories here will appear at the end of the chapter.

We are social creatures, even if we like to be alone most of the time. It is important to take time for yourself as well as making time to connect with others and the world. If you are not connecting with others personally, then connect through causes. The first category dealing with other people is your social life.

BEING OR GETTING SOCIAL

"A healthy social life is found only when, in the mirror of each soul, the whole community finds its reflection, and when, in the whole community, the virtue of each one is living."

—RUDOLF STEINER

Here are the four questions to ask yourself about this category:

1. What's true for me right now in this category?

2. What is my ideal vision in this category?

3. What are the reasons I want to achieve my ideal vision?

4. How the hell am I going to get there?

Do you have friends or people you do social things with, like dinners, celebrations, or vacations? Are there people you consider friends even if you don't see them very often? Do you go to the movies? Do you have lunches with people? Maybe you are an introvert and aren't comfortable with large groups of people. All good.

You've probably read the articles about how important it is to have social connections when you get older. Well, I have read those too, but I prefer to be alone most of the time. Just hanging out here being an introvert. You are probably wondering how I have so many wonderful friends and acquaintances if I am alone most of the time and I'm an introvert to boot. I don't see people very often, but when I do it is "Whoop-dee-do!" and "Here's to ya!" for a rousing good time. Sometimes these get-togethers are totally spontaneous, particularly when I travel or go to lectures or events. And sometimes they are a result of serendipity, pure and simple. Many times, people have leaned over and talked to me when I was in a restaurant by myself, and that led to doing other things together.

What about being social with people through one of your hobbies? I am always bumping into people when I am out birding or standing in line at a book signing or wandering through a market, staring at something. A good skill to learn when you are an introvert is how to become an extrovert on demand. If I am on a long flight and someone next to me just radiates adventure and mystery, then you can bet your bootie I will become Miss Opportunity if that person wants to talk with me.

Here are some great conversation starters for you introverts:

Talk about anything food-related. Humans LOVE food, if you haven't noticed already. We spend hours thinking about what we want to eat next or reading cookbooks to find a recipe worth making. Our lives revolve around satisfying our hunger, and everyone's inner foodie quickly comes out when you bring up the topic. Food bonds people, too, so don't hesitate to mention your favorite restaurant or the latest cake you made, share baking tips, or even share something you baked, if the opportunity arises.

Ask where they're from. Most of the time, people love to talk about their hometown. If it happens that they hated where they grew up, your conversation might segue into other topics, such as travel, where they moved to after college, or what city they like best. You can talk about your hometown, too, and maybe include some interesting or funny stories about your stomping grounds. In my opinion, travel is always, always on people's vision board!

Pets or cute animals will do the trick! Even if you don't have pets, talking about animals (especially cute, furry, funny, fuzzy ones) is a surefire way to get people talking. Most of us have a soft spot for animals, and what makes this topic even more awesome is that there are so many different types of creatures to have a conversation about!

These are three of many conversation starters you can have in your bucket. You will need these or others as you move to include more connection in your kick-ass life. Connected people make more memories, bond, have better moments, and the list goes on. I'm not saying you can't have these on your own, but if you want kick-ass, then start to envision being more connected.

If you have piles of social friends, then keep stacking them up and enjoy every minute.

FINANCES

"Money is a terrible master but an excellent servant."

—P. T. BARNUM

Here are the four questions:

1. What's true for me right now in this category?

2. What is my ideal vision in this category?

3. What are the reasons I want to achieve my ideal vision?

4. How the hell am I going to get there?

Finances often get lumped together with career, from the time we get out of school until we retire, but for our purposes, let's separate them. You wouldn't be reading this if you planned on being a burden to society, which means you should think about what you need to do now, how to leverage what you have, know, and can foresee doing in the future. You need a plan, not just a continued visit to thinking this over.

Because we are talking about the second half of your life, and you plan on a long and healthy journey, it is good to remember that many people who might be financial advisors really don't know how to advise you on something they don't understand or necessarily believe. If you have a relationship with a financial planner and are jumping up and down with the results you are getting and LOVE all of the decisions they make for you, then hell yes, stick with them. If not, make a change now and start the transition plan today!

Taking care of your finances also means that you need to know and plan what you want to do with any money left over when you transition over to whatever you plan to do after this life. Do you need a power of attorney at some point to pay your bills and make decisions? Who would that be and what would you want them to do? Write down your answers, think about them, and maybe talk this over with the person you have in mind.

Another important consideration is your will. If you have things (money, property, personal belongings, etc.) that you want to give away after you die, you will need a will. You can get a template for free online and make a will yourself, or if you choose, you can get a lawyer who specializes in wills and trusts to draft one for you.

If you do have a will, look it over every year when you are going over all of the categories of your life. Things change, as you well know. Possessions come and go. People come and go. Circumstances come and go, so why should your will remain static?

We are part of the first large group of people who will live to be over one hundred, and that isn't something financial planners or insurance agents have figured out yet. How could they? So it is up to us to plan for our longer life and to make sure we have what we need. Are you in the United States? Well, we all know the difficulty Social Security is having keeping up with the numbers of people over sixty depending on it, which means it is best not to count on this for your major financial needs.

If you have stocks, are you investing in things you believe in? If you own property, is it kept up and beneficial to the people using it? I had some excellent financial managers overseeing the small amount of money I had, and yes, my portfolio grew the recommended amount, and all was good. Except...

Except I didn't like the stocks in which they had me invested. Sometimes I disliked the product itself. Sometimes I disliked the CEO and the size of his salary in relation to the profit margin. Sometimes I disliked the board of directors. All old white men? Red flag. All old white men with one woman who had a junior position? Two red flags. Smoke and mirrors. CEO trying to cover up major problems in the annual address to stockholders? Thumbs down. Manipulating the annual report to look good when it is a pile of shit? Not okay.

I had to take charge, jump up and down, and finally take over myself, as I couldn't get my point across. Their job was to make money. Period. I had other ideas.

I didn't do this alone. I took classes for two years so I would be able to make educated and impactful decisions about where I wanted my money to grow. So if you give a damn about your money and what it is doing in the world, do some homework.

I spend about twenty to thirty hours researching a company before I plunk my money down. Start by looking over where you have money invested and see if your investments fit with your moral compass and what you plan on doing with your money during this next period of your life.

If you are all about the bottom-line and don't give a rat's ass about what damage a company is doing, stop reading right here and toss the book in the fire, as you will not be happy with the direction this guidebook takes.

Now, if you already have money and a budget all set up, how are you making that work for you? Are you still paying for things you don't use or want any more, like subscriptions or software or donations to organizations that your priorities no longer align with? Look through your credit card statements and your checking account, and see if there are things you are paying for that you totally forgot about. If so, make the necessary corrections.

Don't hold back. Make it a big, hairy, scary audacious goal. And remember, this isn't set in stone. This is a first step.

CAREER

"Whether you think you can or you think you can't, you're right."

—HENRY FORD

Here are the four questions:

1. What's true for me right now in this category?

2. What is my ideal vision in this category?

3. What are the reasons I want to achieve my ideal vision?

4. How the hell am I going to get there?

This whole section could be called "jobs" or "profession" or "career," or even an unknown word we haven't described yet. Basically, it covers what we will be doing to earn money and contribute to the greater good. This earning can be passive or active.

Many of you reading this might already be retired and looking at other possibilities. Great! Doesn't matter where you are in the scheme of things. In a kick-ass life, you will have the opportunity for a second kick-ass career or contribution of your time and talents.

What I have found is that people over sixty are starting businesses right and left, and their new careers don't resemble anything close to what they did before. They have a new reason (their "why") for what they are doing, and their entire strategy is different. No longer are they trying to raise the kids or pay off the mortgage or climb the ladder.

Other people I have talked with are continuing their career by consulting or advising or bringing in family members and expanding. This could be a big area, and now is the perfect time to dream of possibilities and have fun with it.

Reflect on what career and job mean to you. If you have never had a career but worked your butt off doing different jobs, then go with that and look at what you know about jobs you have held. What could you do with regard to career and jobs in this second half of your life? Did you spend years doing something that benefited others? Could you teach others? Could you write a manual?

Then think about things you really like doing for no other reason than you just frickin' like them.

I had a dear friend who was the best cook. He could whip up dinners for two or twenty-two that would take your breath away. He had a half-assed kitchen about the size of two postage stamps where miracles happened.

When he was seventy-eight, he told me he always wanted to be a chef. Well, damn. Why didn't he pursue that? I never knew. Don't do that to yourself.

Don't give a twit about what other people might say about your choice because some people think what they say matters a big damn, but little do they know they are just nattering on and probably jealous. Envy or fear is usually the main reason why people share their opinions or can't shut their big mouths.

I read a story recently about a retired professional basketball player who is now a crossing guard at an elementary school. He loves it but gets criticized all the time for doing something other people think he shouldn't be doing. Well, eff them. This second half of life is for you and not what others might think you should be doing.

People have told me amazing stories about career or job changes, and all of these changes made the people bright-yellow happy. I know a woman who was a gynecologist and chose to be a community theater actress, and another who was an attorney and gave it up to be a flower shop owner.

I've met several people who turned their hobbies into sweet little businesses and called their own shots, and I've met inventors who no longer have to turn over their creative masterpieces to companies they worked for.

My point is that the second-half-of-lifers are an amazing group of people who have so much energy and enthusiasm for whatever it takes to be successful (on our terms) with new interests and income streams. Give yourself permission to dream big, and write down all of the possibilities and how you could go about making them a reality. Start small but dream big.

QUALITY OF LIFE

"The quality of our life is directly proportional to the quality of our thoughts."

—AVIJEET DAS

Your quality of life is a place to take a deep breath, a place to go for refuge. Here are the four questions to look at:

1. What's true for me right now in this category?

2. What is my ideal vision in this category?

3. What are the reasons I want to achieve my ideal vision?

4. How the hell am I going to get there?

Some people want to downsize and live in a smaller place now that their family is no longer living with them. But I have met others who are now recently remarried, and they want a big house so both families can come together in one place.

My quality of life includes abundance and sharing. Not necessarily abundance of money (although that helps), but abundance of experiences and time spent with family and friends. I also want an abundance of laughter and feeling lighter.

In terms of things, I want an electric car and to continue my life as a minimalist, which means a small house, preferably in the woods. Lately, I've also been wanting a dog or maybe two. A rescue dog. What about you? Oh, the things you can do with a dog...or dogs. They bring such joy. Okay, back to my point...

Things have been complicated for quite a while now, so I am looking for simplicity and a sense of calm. I do have my list of places I want to visit and things I want to see, which include seeing the heavens through one of the world's large telescopes and seeing the aurora borealis. What are you dreaming about?

And I want to go on safari and snorkel with sea turtles and see birds in Madagascar. Far flung, out of the way, and wild.

I experimented by living and traveling in a seventeen-foot travel trailer from one side of the country to the other. I did it four times, and I want to report that the country is beautiful and waiting to be explored if you are so inclined. I will be happy to give you tips about how to make the most of being a vagabond.

I've met many people who live in one place for half of the year and their home country the other half. It seems to work for them. And these are people from Germany, Denmark, Italy, Spain, Australia, and India, just to name a few, so it isn't just people in the US or Canada who do this to escape the winters or, in some cases, the heat of the summer.

Take some time now, put the book down, and ponder these four questions about where you are now, where you want to be, the reasons to achieve your ideal vision, and why and how you will make that happen. Take your time with this and maybe write your answers as bullet points to begin with. Give yourself permission to get in touch with what is important to you.

RELATIONSHIPS OUTSIDE OF FAMILY

"When you stop expecting people to be perfect, you can like them for who they are."

—DONALD MILLER

Here are the four questions as a guideline:

1. What's true for me right now in this category?

2. What is my ideal vision in this category?

3. What are the reasons I want to achieve my ideal vision?

4. How the hell am I going to get there?

This area definitely includes people you would call friends, but it also includes associates from groups you belong to, teammates, business contacts, employees, and maybe even your attorney and accountant. Maybe you see them once a year or more often, but you still have a relationship with them.

Based on my reading and observations about myself and others, I believe the old saying that "blood is thicker than water" changes as we age to "friendship is thicker than water," and I know one thing for sure: friends can influence our happiness and habits. One of the keys to keeping friendships in good working order is to repair, renew, and when needed, replace.

Strong family ties are important, make no mistake about that. But many people do not have family nearby, or they aren't close to their family like they are to their friends. On a darker note, strains on friendships can be negative to our health as we age, so move away from friendships that drag you down a path you don't like anymore.

If you have friends who drink too much, complain all the time, or gossip a lot, let them go. It is best to spend your time investing in friendships that encourage you to stay healthy, mentally and physically. You truly do become who you hang out with. Science proves this, and well...just ponder who you are currently hanging out with. Ask yourself what your results are in life right now.

Sometimes you don't have a choice about spending time with friends, as people you know move, divorce, or die, and you find you need to reach out and find new friends. Community organizations, volunteer work, and religious groups offer new friendship possibilities.

I recently read about a group called Bloomingdale Aging in Place, which was started in 2009 by residents of a neighborhood in New York. According to their website, they now have over one thousand members and over fifty activity groups in categories like exercise and wellness; dining, cooking, outings, and more; art, pastimes, business, and more; and reading. I thought the group that visits dive bars sounded interesting.

Another way friendships are forming is through groups of people sharing a house together. So far, I only know of groups of women doing this, but I am sure there are couples and men and others doing the same thing. Everyone in the house has chores, shares cooking and shopping duties, and of course helps pay the bills. Multigenerational groups can live together too, even if they are not related.

CONTRIBUTION TO SOCIETY

"There is no greater calling than to serve your fellow men. There is no greater contribution than to help the weak. There is no greater satisfaction than to have done it well."

—**WALTER REUTHER**

As a reminder, here are the four questions:

1. What's true for me right now in this category?

2. What is my ideal vision in this category?

3. What are the reasons I want to achieve my ideal vision?

4. How the hell am I going to get there?

What are you going to leave as a legacy? Boom, another hard-hitting question, but probably the most important one in this entire book. This category is very important to me because I believe that everyone has abilities and gifts and contributions to make to themselves, their family, and their community. People who are connected to others and their communities feel powerful, respected, and valued.

We haven't come this far to sit back and let society fumble around when we know damn well we can do something to make things better for everyone. I'm aware of the controversy in the contribution area. What the hell? You've been giving back since you were eleven years old.

Working your butt off delivering papers, helping at home, taking care of your siblings, working hard to get good grades, working while going to college, raising kids, taking care of your family, and helping your parents and grandparents. What's all this about contribution? Are you exhausted? Enough is enough, right?

I get it, and yes, you deserve to curl up and have a nice glass of whatever, read a book, relax on the beach, putter in your garage, and say no more. Yes, you have done enough. Paid your taxes, voted, returned your library books, kept your yard looking nice, bought Girl Scout cookies (I love the mint ones), helped out with the school, coached a Little League team, and made hundreds of other "contributions" that made society better.

Thank you very much. Truly, you have done enough. But not everyone had that opportunity, and some who did still feel the spark when they help someone else. So definitely do NOT feel like you need to do anything here at all; in fact, you can just skip this part and move on.

If you have that yearning to do more moving forward, then think about things you love to do.

Reflect on your contribution to society. What talents do you have? What interests do you have? What do you believe about giving back? What kinds of things would you like to do to help others?

Do you have something to contribute, like a collection of stamps, some artwork, or maybe a library? Do you want to offer your skills or donate or raise money? What is your mental image of someone you respect who gives freely and still has lots of time for themselves and their goals?

Think of the reasons why giving is so important. Did people help you when you were younger? Did your parents help others? Do you have friends who give back that you could talk to? Have you been in a situation where helping others made a difference in someone's life? How did that feel? I know many people my age who would love to contribute in some way but don't know how to get started. They feel they wouldn't be good enough or know enough, but that is a load of crap. There are tons of people out there waiting to be asked, so why not contribute by asking others and telling people about opportunities that you know about?

If you were an activist before you reached sixty, then chances are you are still an activist. Many people want to see changes in social justice. There are activists for climate change and sound democracy. There are immigration activists, peace activists, and education activists. There are environmental and animal rights activists.

Being an activist is one way to make a difference. I lived in a mountain village in Mexico where the people very actively gave back. The residents did this in many ways, from buying shoes for kids so they could attend school to picking up trash to teaching women how to set up cooperatives to setting up a cooking school for young chefs. But the activists I loved the most were the ones who set up free spay-and-neuter programs to reduce the number of stray dogs and cats.

In addition, there were those who set up shelters and adoption programs. If someone who had pets died, they would take the pets in. Wow, just wow. What a cause. If someone got sick and couldn't care for their pets, they offered foster care. They found shelters in the US that no longer had animals turned in because their spay-and-neuter programs had been so successful. They found a way to get dogs to those places so they could find their forever home.

There were veterinarians who gave the dogs shots and neutered or spayed them. There were people who donated property for the shelter, people who donated supplies and built kennels, and of course, volunteers who took care of the animals by feeding, cleaning, and exercising them.

There were people who volunteered to fly to the US with the animals and meet the shelter staff on the other end. There were people who would pick up the crates the animals flew in and drive them back across the border to be used again. This wasn't a one-person operation. A great many people were involved in one way or another. They held fundraisers all the time with people gifting musical talent, artwork, vacation homes, and so on. Together, they made a difference, and so can we all.

You can also give something personal that you have or that was given to you. I recently read about a man named Albert Fischer who has given blood every fifty-six days for over sixty years or, if years are a blur, since Harry Truman was president. Holy crap. That's a long time!

But he isn't the only one. There are people who have collected for years and then find themselves wondering what to do with all of their hard work when they have to downsize or move. Think about donating your collection.

My mother gave me a number of very old logging photos from the Mount Rainier area where her father logged at the beginning of the 1900s, and I carried them around from move to move across the country and back and then realized they would be of immense value to a museum or historical society. I really couldn't even identify my grandfather in the photos, so they didn't mean a great deal to me. Now they have a proper home and can be a source of history for many people rather than being stuffed in a box.

I have a dear friend who is an excellent listener. I mean 100 percent all the time. This is an amazing gift, and she shares it all the time. People feel safe talking with her, and they feel appreciated and respected too. I know when I talk with her, I always feel lighter and like someone finally heard me. If you are able to do that, then find a way to be with people who need to be listened to. It will change their lives.

There are people in their nineties teaching yoga and tai chi. Attorneys, coaches, therapists, mentors, teachers, and musicians all continue working and contributing and challenging the regular norms of retirement. I have a friend whose retired hairdresser comes to her house and cuts her hair in the driveway while they catch up on what's happening. He still keeps a few clients, but now it is on his schedule.

I have another friend who packs her scissors when she vacations in Mexico and cuts hair for the women in the village where she stays.

There are also opportunities for longer-duration volunteering, which are something to look into if that interests you and you have the time. I went into the Peace Corps when I was sixty-three and taught at a university in Ukraine for two years. It was an amazing experience for me. I had traveled a lot but had never worked in another country, which is a whole other layer of being immersed in a different culture while providing a service.

I was recently talking with a man who built houses in other countries with Habitat for Humanity and others who have built schools or dug wells or figured out ways to get clean water to remote villages. Not everyone can or chooses to leave their home environment for an extended time, but if you have ever thought of it, reexamine it now for possibilities.

I visited the Vietnam Veterans Memorial a while back, and my tour was at night. Sitting there in his wheelchair, in the dark with just the lights from the memorial shining on him, was a veteran volunteering to talk to anyone about the memorial, someone they knew, or what the symbols next to the names meant; he would also help them find a loved one's name on the wall.

We talked for a long time, and he told me he had been going there for years because he felt connected to the people on the wall and wanted to be a living representative of that war. It was his way. Because of him, I looked into other ways people could help veterans and found out there are volunteer opportunities at USOs, veterans' hospitals, and senior centers.

Sometimes it is helping fill out paperwork coming from the government, which, as you know, can be overwhelming. Sometimes it is talking and listening and seeing what needs to be done. This is especially necessary if the person has vision or hearing difficulties.

If plants and gardening are a passion for you, think about becoming a Master Gardener. It is a long program but well worth it. What is more satisfying than seeing things grow and helping people learn about the joy of gardening and making things beautiful? I did it, and it sure didn't feel like work when I was spending time with plants and helping people with their questions.

There are a lot of opportunities in this area, and people are hungry to find answers to their questions. You could be the person with those answers. You get the idea. There are so many opportunities, and with the talents and skills you have learned, developed, and practiced over the years, you are the perfect choice to share that information.

Once again, do not take my word for it because each person is unique in what interests them, and this is the time to do or not to do exactly what works for you without any pressure from society, family, church, work, or anything else. Be curious and have fun.

We're doing some great work. How do you feel? I told you we'd do some difficult work but have fun doing it. Next, I'm going to teach you ways to get some of your valuable time back so you have even more time for your important contributions *and* fun.

THOUGHT EXERCISE / ACTION STEP

Recall the four "mapping your vision" questions.

1. Start with what's true about yourself right now. Find out what your beliefs and assumptions are for each category. What is the concept and mental image you have of yourself in each area? Write out where you are currently at.

2. Next, write out how you see yourself in your ideal way.

3. Write out the reasons behind what you want to do in each category.

4. Finally, how the hell are you going to get there?

Use those four questions to define and map your vision in each of these main categories:

- Social

- Financial

- Career

- Quality of life

- Relationships outside of family

- Contribution to society

Also add or subtract any categories that don't apply to you or that you find unnecessary.

YOUR KICK-ASS MANTRA

"Today, I am perfect. So is my kick-ass vision!"

Chapter 5

WHAT'S TIME GOT TO DO WITH IT?

Feeling good so far? I sure hope so, because you have been working your butt off if you've been keeping up or even simply thinking about how to recalibrate your life so you can be creative, find your purpose, and lead a peak performance life (AKA your kick-ass life).

As a quick reminder, all of this work is going to take time. You might be thinking that you are already at your max schedule limit and that you have zero time left over. Well, that should tell you something, and it might actually be the very reason that you are here.

You hardly have time to pee after dealing with the family, tending to your hobbies, keeping up the house, and trying to make a little money on the stock market. What is this woman talking about? Whoa, my new friend, don't shoot the messenger.

I have written this book because I have been there and done that. I am also living my dream life at the age of seventy-six, and it is kick-ass! If you don't have a ton of leftover time, then you definitely have not made time for things that really matter to you.

We have twenty-four hours in a day. We need to sleep for a third of that, so basically, we have about sixteen hours a day to get shit done, meditate, and throw in some mantras. No problem, plenty of time.

Here is my daily kick-ass schedule as an example:

> 5:30–7:30 a.m. Out of bed. Start the coffee. Check the list I made the night before. Twenty minutes of qigong, fifteen minutes of meditation, reading material outside my comfort zone—usually science, technology, or investing. Do strength exercises. Five-minute gratitude journal.

> 7:30–8:30 a.m. Walking.

> 8:30–8:45 a.m. Check the stock market (I'm currently on Central time) and email. I don't answer any email at this time.

> 8:45–9:30 a.m. Work period, usually writing.

> 9:30–10:00 a.m. Breakfast.

> 10:00–11:30 a.m. Work period.

> 11:30 a.m.–12:30 p.m. Phone calls, emails, short errands, check my trades.

> 12:30–2:00 p.m. Work period.

2:00–4:00 p.m. Editing, planning next day, research.

Stop work at 4:00 p.m.

Evening consists of second walk, dinner, reading, and errands or chores.

I have three work periods in my day, and sometimes those are Zoom calls with my writing groups or my business associates. I count those as work too. I often work on Saturday or Sunday and take a day during the week to take care of paperwork, grocery shopping, banking, and so on.

I'm big on recovery, so once a month, I take a whole weekend off, do something totally different, and don't even think about working at all. And that includes a long hike or two. Once every three months, I will take about five days and go somewhere or work on other things I love doing, like art and photography.

Was I always this organized? Hell no. And even now, I take mental health days and just become a blank slate. On those days, lettuce looks smart compared to me. It took me years to get where I am now, and I wouldn't be here at all if I hadn't found a purpose. I had to wade through everything I talk about in this book and dig myself out of denial with my bare hands many times. This won't happen overnight.

Are you the opposite when it comes to time? Already super productive and get everything done quickly? Let's look at whether you are truly being productive or you are just busy. You can spend all day running around, doing errands, fixing this or that, making plans, making endless lists, checking your email, answering the phone, and dealing with the repair people only to find at the end of the day that you didn't accomplish any of the things you really intended to. This crosses over into both areas, productivity and busyness. But separate out what you could have delegated on this type of day. Yes, you did do things, but were they the things that really mattered or were you just super busy? In my experience and opinion, if you can delegate and be productive with what you really want to be doing every day, that is a kick-ass win! By being productive, you also inch yourself toward your goals every single day, doing something that brings you closer bit by bit.

BE PRODUCTIVE, NOT BUSY

Say you want to send out a flyer to all of your customers telling them about your flower sale. A productive person might do the following:

Step 1. Decide on the date, time, and what flowers and plants you are going to have for sale. Make sure appropriate staff is scheduled.

Step 2. Look at flyer templates on Word and figure out which one you want to use. Get all the photos you want on the desktop of your computer. Watch a YouTube video about making flyers.

Step 3. Write out everything you want to go into the flyer, such as the headline, location, hours, where to park, plants and flowers available, and pricing. Select bonuses and prizes to be given out during the day.

Step 4. Fill in the template with the photos, and cut and paste the narrative. Make corrections if necessary, and send it out to your mailing list.

This is the way to take action and get results. Maybe it isn't the fanciest flyer out there. Maybe it isn't perfect, but it gets the job done and informs potential customers.

Now a busy person (and I have been one of these a lot, so I speak from experience) will start doing research on various types of flyers and which format to use. They will look into what mailing service to use and how many photos should be included. Then they will call three people to find out what they think and who to hire to make it look really professional, and on and on, making list after list.

The bottom line is that busy people overthink things a lot. Most are referred to as perfectionists. Nothing is ever, ever going to be perfect! Busy people usually expand what they do to fill up the entire amount of time they have available. Busy people are great at "looking busy" while productive people are getting results.

Busy people cram as much as they can into their day, while productive people always look at ways to make their to-do list smaller. The moment I really got this, my life forever changed. I mean, I really, truly delegated, removed items from my list, and removed the busyness.

Busy people get distracted easily and try to do more and more, while productive people learn damn quickly the difference between urgent and important. Busy people get blindsided by urgent concerns that gobble up their time, while productive people learn to tell the difference between important and unimportant tasks and focus on doing what matters.

Busy people have found hundreds of ways to reduce what they get done by doing mundane things that seem important but really aren't. Productive people create systems for dealing with things that can be distractions, like emails and phone calls. They set aside specific times to deal with those, leaving the rest of their time to do what needs to be done.

Busy people often seem tired, frustrated, and burdened by putting out fires, while productive people know when to take a break by going for a walk or getting a drink of water or just staring out the window for a few minutes. Productive people know they can achieve greater results when they let their brain take a break. The list goes on, but enough for now. You get it, right?

THOUGHT EXERCISE / ACTION STEP

Figure out what kind of a person you are: productive or just busy. Decide whether or not you want to do anything about it. If you feel that things are going great, then carry on. If you don't like what happens to your time, then you have some choices to make.

TIME MANAGEMENT

What about time management? Can you truly manage time? The truth is that you can only manage yourself, and this will require a lot of work. In the fifties and sixties, time management was based on efficiency as well as new tools and technology in the home and workplace that would help us do things faster. If we did things faster, we would have more time.

Wouldn't we? Did it really work? In the late eighties, along came Dr. Stephen Covey and his seven habits, and we learned the difference between urgency and importance so we could prioritize. We still do that today by putting what matters the most at the top of the list.

I get that; I used to do that all the time, but it didn't help me get more time or figure out a way to get the rest of my damn list done. So, if efficiency is like getting a vacuum cleaner with more suction, then prioritizing is like stealing time from one piggy bank and giving to another without even asking. Rude.

Time management at this point is based on urgency and importance, but there is something else to consider, and that is how long something is going to be of significance. This means we not only ask "What's the most important thing we can do today?" but "What can we do today, right now, to make the future better?"

Procrastination

Now, let's get into the tough conversation: let's talk about procrastination. This is one topic that we cannot skip over.

Everyone procrastinates; it's a way of life. But it really doesn't have to be. There is good procrastination and there is bad.

I used to frequently get awards for procrastinating and wasting time. Maybe you have a couple of those too. Over the years, I have learned a few ways to get back on track more easily and to not lose sight of what I really want to accomplish.

I can throw a tantrum like a two-year-old who doesn't want to go to bed and procrastinates with all kinds of tricks: monsters under the bed, dying of thirst, even looking for a random toy to sleep with that probably never existed. But by doing this work, I have learned to dig a bit deeper.

What is it about a particular task that makes me stall like a stubborn mule? Do I need more information? Have I broken it down into manageable bits? Do I feel like an imposter? Have I set my intention for that particular work period? Can I delegate this part to someone else? Have I made some bad decisions?

These are some types of questions I ask myself, and I realize that most of the procrastination has to do with some kind of fear. So, when I look at what I am doing with a different focus, I can usually pinpoint my problem.

Often, the key is just getting this one thing done so you can jump right to what you really want to be doing. I have to make it some kind of game. There is this newish word out there, "gamification," but it is really a mind game of tricks you learn to play on your stubborn self to keep things moving.

I might say, "Okay you lazy sack of shrimp, work for thirty minutes and then you can read your mystery for thirty minutes" or "Finish that one part and then have a glass of wine." Do whatever it takes to jump over that part you don't like so much to get to the stuff you really enjoy doing.

We know that putting off something necessary that we don't feel like doing and checking our email instead is bad procrastination. This is the enemy of success. But good procrastination is waiting to do something because we have decided, after looking over everything we want to do, that right now isn't the best time.

That rational decision isn't the enemy; it is a virtue. It is hard to perfect the kick-ass art form of patience: the patience to delay, delegate, or just not do the insignificant things. The bottom line is simple. Notice I said simple, but not easy.

Perception of Time

What about our perception of time? We've all had experiences when time seems to fly by: we're having a great dinner conversation with friends, and when we look up, the restaurant is empty, and the waitstaff is sweeping the floor, glaring at us. Where did the time go?

When working on projects I'm totally committed to, the days fly by. There is also the opposite experience, when I don't want to be doing something and the time doesn't seem to move at all. Ever been there? I have waited at signals that I swear were five minutes long—and I did swear too. I've been in meetings that seem to go on forever and nothing at all happens. Yuck. How does this play out in our daily lives? It sucks time from what we could be doing...kicking ass.

Do you know what the Bannister Effect is? Roger Bannister cracked the sub-four-minute mile in May 1954. He was the first person to do it. Doctors thought he might keel over after the race. Runners had been trying to reach this goal for years. It seemed impossible—this was something that couldn't be done. No one could run that fast.

No amount of training, endurance, mojo, or whatever was going to make it happen, but then it *did* happen. Then another amazing thing happened. After the record was broken, another person ran the mile in under four minutes. Then a few more people did the same, and pretty soon records in other races were also falling.

So, what seemed impossible in a given amount of time turned out not only to be possible but became available for others too.

We can shift our thinking on some of the things we have deemed to always take a certain amount of time—maybe reading a book or cleaning the garage or having a meeting with a group of people. If you want more time in your life to do the things that please you and bring you pleasure, then you will need to find ways to change your perception of how much time it takes to do something and set a new challenge.

I write short articles. There have been times that one would take me a week to finish, but over time, I have learned to whittle that down to ninety minutes. Now, I aim to do it in even less time. It's a work in progress.

I was falling into Parkinson's law, which states that work expands to fill the time allotted. My writing didn't need to take that much time, but I didn't put any special restraint on myself, so it dragged on and on.

> ## THOUGHT EXERCISE / ACTION STEP
>
> Figure out a reasonable amount of time to do something and get it done in that amount of time.

How to Deal with Time Vampires

Yes, interruptions happen. What the hell can you do about that, huh? What if we learn to make time work to our advantage? It can happen; I have done it.

People interruptions are more difficult to control, but those weren't my biggest offenders. Mine were my iPhone and my computer. Pings, bings, rings, music, you name it. Drove me bonkers.

I turn my phone to silent so I don't hear any pings when messages come in. I also keep it across the room and not next to me. As much as I love the device, I have to make it work for me. That took some training of other people (think daughters) who thought I was their personal assistant and should be available twenty-four/seven.

Also, because I give to a lot of my favorite causes, they think I am a wallet at their disposal. The Do Not Call List doesn't apply to political calls or nonprofits, so I get tons of those calls too. I NEVER answer a call unless the caller is in my contacts. I've made lots of calls as a volunteer for this or that organization, and we never left messages, so I can pretty much tell who is trying to reach me. And 99 percent of the time, the caller doesn't leave a message.

I also turned off all notifications on my computer so I don't get those little pop-ups in the top right of my screen anymore. I also had to get control of the seemingly endless stream of emails I receive. In comes a neat little app called Unroll.me.

On the front end, you have to tell it where to put your emails. You can put them in the rollup, unsubscribe, or leave them in your email inbox. Then the little AI dudes figure you out and start asking you where you want things to be. You can always switch out from one category or another. Now, once a day I get this Unroll.me email with messages from all of the companies I used to get emails from. I can look at them at a glance and choose to read or not. My inbox has maybe five emails.

I also love the unsubscribe feature because I get damn tired of organizations asking me if I really want to unsubscribe and why and maybe I don't and "click this button if you changed your mind" and holy shit! Just take me off the damn list already!

Now Unroll.me does it. Delegated. Done.

THOUGHT EXERCISE / ACTION STEP

Identify your time vampires. Develop an action plan for dealing with them. Delegate if necessary.

FOCUS YOUR ENERGY AND ATTENTION

In addition to time, we also have energy and attention. We can have a bright shiny day in front of us with a clean slate and all things brushed aside, but what happens if we didn't sleep well or we have to plan a big dinner party by yesterday? Oops. That time we had sort of slips off into the muck of reality.

So, besides time, we always need to be focusing our energy and attention if we expect to accomplish our goals. Damn, this sounds like a lot of work. Well, yes and no. Some work now for a lot of free time later. Sounds like a good trade-off, wouldn't you agree?

And there you go with your attention drifting off to that vacation again. Soon you will have the time you need to take one.

First, take a look at your routines. Simplify and systematize where you can. Morning and evening. How much time are you devoting to what you do in the morning? Is everything you want to wear laid out and ready to put on? Is the coffee ready to go by just pushing a button?

Do you have everything you need for a nice shower all ready and nearby? Do you know where everything is that is part of your morning routine? Do you know how much time each part takes to do? For example, how much time do you spend in the shower? Ten minutes? Time it. Then say you will do your shower in four minutes and set the timer. How will you get a ten-minute shower done in four minutes? Hmmmm. Get creative.

Let me tell you my four minutes story. I was in Australia at a camping place, and the showers cost fifty cents for four minutes.

Then the water shut off and you had to step out and put in another fifty cents. The coin depository wasn't right outside of the shower, so you couldn't just step out; you had to walk across the room...naked and wet. What a pain!

I learned damn quick how to shower in four minutes. Are there times when I want to hang out in the shower and think? You bet. But not every day and not every shower. My point is that you should look over your routine and see if there are ways you can make it better and not take so much time; make it a game. Remember: gamification.

Do the same with your evening routine. Be sure to plug in all of your devices and shut off your screens an hour before bedtime. If you use your phone as an alarm clock, turn it over so you do not see the screen. These little habit shifts will add up over time. Trust me.

Here are two simple things to incorporate into your evening routine: (1) write out your productive to-do list for the next day and (2) write in your gratitude journal. Some of the most powerful gratitude entries I do involve listing the top things that have irritated me that week or even day, then writing out why I am grateful for those irritations.

This does wonders, especially if you end up writing things about yourself that irritated you. Gratitude will disarm these inconveniences or thoughts almost instantly. You can also try a pre-sleep gratitude routine: think about something that worked really well and went just as you planned, why that happened, and why you are grateful for it. Drift off to those pleasant thoughts and you will be ready for the next day.

The things that kill my time are usually those things I cannot control very well, like grocery shopping and doing errands. Things that involve traffic, lots of people, and unknowns. I put "NEVER go shopping for groceries on a Saturday" on my "never do again" list.

Instead, I go on Tuesday. The trucks are unloaded on Monday, and by Tuesday things are looking good. Try grocery shopping at 8:00 a.m. or 7:00 p.m., by yourself if possible. You do have a "never do again" or "things that can save you time and frustration list," don't you? Don't worry, I'll include it in the thought exercise / action step.

Writing down all of these thoughts and plans is what causes a shift or set of shifts in your life. Just thinking about something isn't enough, because this doesn't give your words power. The written word does. The action of pausing to write these things out is what can completely change your life and your results.

By the way, if shopping is your entertainment and fills you with joy, then what can I say? This is one of your joyful times, so go for it! Just be sure you figure out better and more efficient ways to do every single thing you do, manage, or handle in life.

I read about this game recently (I cannot remember the source, but thank you) where every day, the bank deposits $86,400 into your account. However, you have to spend the money within the day and cannot move it to another account. What is left over gets removed at the end of the day, but lo and behold, another $86,400 shows up the next day.

The bank can decide at any time to stop the game without warning. So, what would you do in this situation? Would you go out and start buying everything you want for yourself and those you love and care about? Would you start investing like crazy? Here's the deal: you actually do get 86,400 deposited each day, but they are seconds of time, not dollars. Yes, they are a gift, and you will make a humungous difference in your life if you use them wisely.

Remember that the lists you are making regarding how you deal with your time are like a big vault. You take the things out of your head that you want to do and put them on these lists. Not every fricking thing, for Pete's sake! Start with four to five really important things you want to do and increase to six maximum.

Any more than that and you won't complete it, meaning you won't get that little squirt of feel-good stuff that happens when you complete something. Once your list is on paper, you free up your brain to think about other things. All you have to do is look at the list and you know exactly what you are doing first, second, and so on, and as Brian Tracy, a Canadian-American motivational speaker and author of over eighty books, says, "Eat the ugly frog first."

Do the biggest, most difficult, and most important thing first while you still have momentum. That also frees up a lot of brain space for other thinking. It seems we have quite a bit of willpower in the morning, but as the day goes on, it fades, so look at that list and get busy!

I remember training for marathons. If I didn't do my running early in the morning (sometimes around 4:00 a.m.), life would get in the way. I'd need to do things with the kids, and the running wouldn't happen. On the few occasions when it did,

I was tired and didn't feel like running, even though I knew I needed to for the training. I was willing to get up early, go out, run those twenty miles, and be home before the house woke up, so that was me eating my ugly frog first. But that frog turned into a nice cup of coffee and a great start to the day.

I wish the morning lasted twenty-four hours because that is when I get my best work done. I write early in the morning and walk afterwards when I need a break. This will be different for everyone. I am a lark (I like to get up early), but some people are night owls and do their best work later in the evening.

What's important here is to find out what works best for you and to move in that direction as soon as you can figure out a way to incorporate that into your life while considering the people you live with.

Chunking things down is really valuable! Think about it: if you do small amounts every day, week, month, and year and then look back, you will be astounded at what you accomplished. What's that saying? How do you eat an elephant? One bite at a time—each day is a bite or two. And there is that quote from Bill Gates that "we always overestimate the change that will occur in the next two years and underestimate the change that will occur in the next ten. Don't let yourself be lulled into inaction."

If you put too many things on your list, you won't feel a sense of satisfaction in finishing the list. It is also important to be able to finish the list each day before going to bed, which you can accomplish with four to six items. Try this out and see what works for you. You can always add more, but keep your word to yourself and do not go to bed until everything for that day is finished.

THOUGHT EXERCISE / ACTION STEP

1. Examine your routines (e.g., morning, evening). What can you do to save yourself time? Write these things down and then do them.

2. Make a list of things to never do again.

3. Make a list of what you want to do with your 86,400 seconds of time each day.

LIVE THE LIFE YOU WANT TO LIVE

Have you timed how many hours a week you are working, from the time you leave the house and go to your office or sit at your home office desk? This also means counting when you think about work, handle your emails from your phone, or do some research tied to your work. Are you counting getting ready for work too? Driving to and from work, working at home, and having conversations about work over dinners and with family and friends? Take a minute and figure this out. It is a good exercise because I bet it is way more hours than you might have thought.

If you can learn to cap your hours at thirty-five per week, those extra five hours can be utilized for so many other kick-ass activities. Remember, this is time you are getting to live the life you want to live.

I bet you will find even more than five extra hours a week when you start to say no as well. There are creative ways to say no that work really well, and we need a few of those in the old grab bag. Look at and decide who or what you want to say NO to. You have to have a strategy and be prepared; this is the most important breakthrough in becoming a no-er.

First and foremost, before saying no in the beginning, just buy yourself more time. Don't feel that you have to give an answer right away, even if it is your mother asking. Even if you always say yes.

Surprise the hell out of them and say, "For some reason, that date sounds suspicious. I may already have a commitment. I will check and get back to you." Or you can simply let them know that you will have to get back to them with an answer. You don't owe anyone an explanation. A simple "No, I cannot attend" or "No, I cannot commit to that at this time" will do the trick. If you want to pad it, you can always throw in a "My apologies and thank you for thinking of me, but I won't be able to." Do you get the idea?

One of the biggest time killers is one that we, as humans, all know. Any guesses? Yup, stress! According to the American Psychological Association, there are three types of stress: acute stress, episodic acute stress, and chronic stress. Acute stress is like a fight or flight response. It doesn't last very long.

Maybe you remember the terror or delight you felt as you slowly chugged up the long incline on a roller coaster and then were flung down the other side, heart racing, palms sweaty, and scared shitless, or maybe you remember jumping into cold water and every inch of skin shrieking in protest.

This kind of stress doesn't last very long and can actually be helpful in certain situations by keeping you energetic, focused, and alert. Acute stress doesn't do damage like long-term stress does.

Then there is episodic acute stress. This affects people who worry a lot and people who take on too much. If you dig a little deeper, these people usually have a lot of external demands placed on them. You might have experienced this if you have recently downsized and moved, changed jobs, or retired and now have no idea what you are going to do in life.

The real killer is chronic stress. This is when the central stress response system is out of balance. If you often become impatient, frazzled, or extremely cranky over the littlest things, this is a sure sign that you are a chronic stressor! Basically, feeling like crap and being stressed out all the time will ultimately kill you or, at the very least, make you extremely sick and depressed.

The worst part is that when you suffer with chronic stress for a long time, it has the ability to start feeling normal, and when you endure something like this for a long time, you can develop serious health issues. Chronic stress can also be brought on by someone you care about, live with, or work with.

In some ways, I feel a great swath of chronic stress across the world right now. We've all been through and are still going through the pandemic and are experiencing what is called secondary traumatic stress or compassion fatigue. This is especially true for all of the frontline workers and families of victims. However, chronic stress exists across the board in businesses, communities, churches, schools, and anywhere groups of people know and talk to each other. And depending on the circumstances, some people deal with this kind of stress better than others.

Not knowing is also a huge stressor for people. Jobs, health, children, future, and security are all up in the air. Add to that all of the fires, floods, hurricanes, and other natural disasters, and you have to wonder why we all aren't in therapy.

I worry about all of those things too, and there aren't any easy answers. One of the best things we can do is be aware of what is making us stressed and to do something about it up front. Don't wait until the stress grabs you and drags you down. Systematize it just like your other routines.

Here are a few stress-reducing ideas that you can try on to see which one(s) fit.

- Drink some water and a smallish snack, like ten almonds or a piece of fruit.

- Train your eyes using the 20-20-20 rule: every twenty minutes, take a twenty-second break by looking out at a distance of at least twenty feet. You can put an app on your computer or phone as a reminder, and you can click it off if you don't want a break at that time.

- Do ten to twelve minutes of exercise. This helps your brain to work better and improves attention.

- Do a short ten- to twenty-minute meditation. If meditation scares the crap out of you or you aren't interested in it, then a simple five-minute session of visualizing your stress being removed from your body and life will do the trick!

- Go outside for a few minutes in a natural setting. This is especially important if you are working on your computer a lot. Even looking at pictures of nature can be calming.

- Stare out the window or doodle and let your mind wander.

- Color. Crayons can change most any mood for the better.

- Take a short nap, less than forty minutes. Perks you right up. A longer nap messes with your sleep patterns, and then you'll need twenty-four hours to reset things. Shorter is better.

- Talk to someone else in person or on the phone; this reduces your stress and lets you get back to what you were doing feeling better.

- Read or listen to a chapter of your favorite fiction book, which causes a major brain shift to happen.

- Stand up if you are sitting down a lot, or sit down if you have been standing for a long time.

- Laugh. Read some jokes, watch a short video, or read a funny blog. This will give you a little bit of the feel-good drug dopamine.

- Do some breathing exercises. There are many of these. Here are a couple that I like:

  * Box breathing involves breathing in for a count of four, holding for a count of four, breathing out for a count of four, and holding for a count of four, gradually increasing the number.

  * Neurobiologist Andrew Huberman suggests doing two inhales through the nose followed by a long exhale through the mouth. He calls these "physiological sighs." Do these for a couple of minutes once or twice a day.

This is all about rewiring your brain and shaking up your routines, making more space and opening up time to work for you, instead of you working for time. Doing this now will also remove burnout from your life. Stress causes burnout, and that is a roller coaster that you don't want to stand in line for, let alone get on the damn ride. Good vibes and low stress equals kick-ass living.

Are you living the life you want to live? Hopefully, some of the ideas in this chapter help move you in the right direction. Ultimately, though, you'll still have to put in the hard work yourself. In the next chapter, I'll help you gain some ground on the kick-ass journey through wisdom about creativity.

YOUR KICK-ASS MANTRA

"I create my own kick-ass path and walk it with joy and purpose."

Chapter 6

CREATIVITY: WHERE IDEAS HAVE SEX

Now that we have figured out how to make the time that we have work for us, we have more of that elusive gift to look at some ways to tap into our creativity. Let's explore a few current myths about the aging brain and take an in-depth look at creativity and how, as well as when, it shows up. Do you know how to tap into your own genius and pass it along through your actions? Let's get started!

You have probably heard that the aging brain is more distractable and less inhibited than a younger brain. By the way, why are they calling it "the aging brain" now when it has been aging since the womb? Rhetorical question, right? Just so you know, aging brains score really well on IQ tests of general knowledge, vocabulary, and reasoning. So, if you are more distractable, less inclined to give a crap what anyone else thinks, willing to speak up about what you think, and score really well on IQ tests, then you have what it takes to be creative.

Psychologist Lynn Hasher and her group at the University of Toronto discovered in a study that members of the older, distractable group were better able to solve problems presented to them later in the study, which suggests that the aging brain has a broadening focus of attention. This wider attention lets the individual keep lots of different bits of information in mind at the same time. The process of combining this information and seeing patterns is one of the ways creative ideas are born.

This means that older people like us have access to a huge storehouse of knowledge gathered over a lifetime of learning and gaining skills and experience. Combining those bits of smartness into new and original ideas is what the creative brain is all about, and because we have so much knowledge, we are like a fertile garden in spring, just waiting to bloom. Remember, it is never too late to start being creative. Think of Grandma Moses, who didn't start painting until she was in her seventies. Tony Bennett might have left his heart in San Francisco, but he is still showing his paintings at age ninety-five. Benjamin Franklin invented bifocals at age seventy-eight and Frank Lloyd Wright was drafting updated designs for the Guggenheim Museum in New York at ninety.

CREATIVITY FOR THE AGING BRAIN

Creativity is the ability to think about a problem or task in a new, different, or unique way and the ability to use your imagination to think up new ideas. This lets you solve difficult problems or find new and interesting ways to approach a task. You are able to see things from new angles. You can see patterns and make connections to solve problems. You also enjoy and are motivated to try things that haven't been tried before.

Creativity shows up when you have limitations, constraints, restrictions, and obstacles, and haven't we all had those up the wazoo, especially since the pandemic socked us in the gut? We had many fewer resources to work with as the waves of the crisis washed over us and we were all forced to think outside of the box. Sometimes that box was filled with kids, grandkids, pets, and lots of uncertainty, and I know you learned to use what you had in unconventional ways. We all did. The plus of that is that creative limitations allow you to question your own understanding of what resources and materials you do have and what you can and should do with them. When you think creatively, you are often thinking outside the box of normal ideas and solutions and you can perceive things that are not always obvious. If you don't feel you are creative right now, the good news is that creative thinking is a skill you can nurture and develop.

It is normal to think of artistic people as being creative, but there are many other types of creativity, such as planning a dinner for eight or looking at your bare backyard and creating a beautiful garden. When you see fashionable people, this is them tapping into their creativity. We are being creative all the time, but we don't label it that way.

Creative problem solving is another way to think differently; I bet you do it all the time and don't even realize it. You have probably thought about ways to reduce energy use or cut down on throwaway plastic usage, create a budget, or plan a vacation. This is creative problem solving.

Creative thinking can be expressed in several ways. Here are five ways I've identified for you:

1. **Gaining understanding of a problem.** This is
    a super creative process. Before you get to the
    creative part, you need to know just what is going
    on. You need to examine things like you are looking
    through a microscope so you know all the parts and
    can analyze them. Once you have your data, the
    creativity sets in.

2. **Having an open mind.** This is a huge creative
    strength. Set aside all of your previous beliefs
    and any biases you might have and look at things
    with fresh eyes and in a completely new way. By
    having your mind open like a sail in the wind, you
    give yourself the opportunity to think creatively.
    Open-minded people are naturally creative. Closed-
    minded people block their creativity.

3. **Problem solving.** I want to rename this and
    call it "creative solving." When you are thinking
    through different ways to fix or solve something,
    this is creativity working in a huge-ass way. When
    you consider ways you can solve the problem, like
    looking for outside help, navigating to find the right
    tools, or locating someone who has experience with
    similar problems, this. Is. Creative. Thinking.

4. **Getting organized.** Being neat and tidy isn't
    usually connected with creative people. However,
    tidy people have found ways to creatively clean and
    organize their space. Organization isn't just for
    stuff. Getting your ideas organized so other people
    can understand your vision really helps when
    you are asking for advice. Again, this is big-time

creative. Being able to talk with people in a way that lets them see the possibilities is a win for everyone, and this is creativity at its finest.

5. **Communicating effectively.** Lots of people think this means you need to be able to talk and write well, and for the most part it does, but being a good listener is also a huge piece of the creative pie here. Become curious about things, ask a lot of questions, and then learn to listen carefully to the answers— this will often give you the missing puzzle pieces you were looking for to solve a problem as well. Creativity rocks!

There are also some skills we can practice that can make us more creative, like making connections between different ideas. This can be done by reading or listening to people and seeing some link between things, being in a new place, or experiencing something for the first time. Basically, get out of your comfort zone of always doing things the same way with the same people and doing the same activities. That is boring. Creativity instantly kills boring. Boring can't live outside of the comfort zone; it just isn't possible. Creativity thrives outside of boring and outside of the comfort zone. It's science, really.

I am super creative because I ask a ton of questions, all of the time, to almost anyone I meet. It instantly shoves me out of my comfort zone and into the kick-ass creativity of the "anything is possible" zone. Asking a lot of questions sparks a ton of aha moments, especially when you challenge the normal way of looking at something or following certain procedures the same way. Asking why to yourself or others can put you on a whole new track of thinking.

Being observant is another way to link into creativity. Yes, people-watching counts. Observing is another way of getting curious. Get curious about how people use products and services, what people think of them, and so on. Can you see ways to make things better? Aha!!! Creativity lands again! Try experimenting with your own ideas too. Do you have a product or service idea? These ideas might seem weird and unusual at first because, well, most ideas do, but test them out anyway. Invite creativity in; give creativity a seat at the table. Remember that creative people see something not working as an opportunity and not a failure. Remember, Thomas Edison "failed" ten thousand times before he got the light bulb, and we thank him. Need I say more here?

Moving on.

THE POWER OF "YET"

I was at an open house for my grandson's school a couple of years ago, and one of the teachers was explaining how they teach the children a very important word so when they get frustrated and want to give up, the children will remember the word Y-E-T. They just don't understand it *yet*. So remember that little word and give yourself a break when it seems too difficult. Once you dig into all of the areas where you truly are creative, I think you will be surprised at your findings.

I was reading yet another research report recently, from Steven Kotler, author as well as founder and executive director of the Flow Research Collective, regarding creativity. According to his research, "we're trying to train a skill, but what we really need to be training is a state of mind." The difficult problems of today, such as war, poverty, energy shortages, and homelessness need serious creative thinking as well as problem solving and ultimately...responses.

We're used to treating problems with money, time, people, or supplies, but that often breeds corruption or more problems. So how do we go about locating this state of mind? What can we do to get to a place where we can find and explore ideas and creativity? First of all, it is critical that you enjoy, like, and get satisfaction from whatever creative endeavor you are doing. This might take a while, as many people had their creative juices squeezed out of them decades prior by narrow-minded people who thought their way was the right way. You probably remember left-handed people telling you they had their hands hit with rulers so they would use their right hand. Maybe others who painted the sun blue and were given a failing grade because the sun had to be yellow? Yes, sadly, creativity killers are always on the loose. But we need to push forward and keep on keeping on. No matter what. Consider the power of "yet"—as in, we just haven't found a solution *yet*.

DON'T LISTEN TO THE NAYSAYERS

I was listening to a talk from Ken Robinson, a British author and speaker (I miss him a lot; rest in peace, my dear friend) talking about two of the Beatles going to a school across town from his in Liverpool and the music teacher telling them that they had no talent. No talent?! Yikes, glad they didn't listen to that person. And Elvis? He got kicked out of the glee club at his school because the teacher said his voice was so awful. How did that work out for the glee club, I wonder? I'm sure you have many stories of your own and just ended up giving up because some adult (or childhood "friend" or bully) discouraged you with a bad grade or with an offhand remark. Sucks, right? But we are working toward a kick-ass second half, right? So now we move on. Leave that baggage behind, on an island (better yet, a deserted island), never to visit it again. This is where you can say "eff you" to all of those naysayers and get back in touch with whatever it was that set your heart on fire. After all, this is about the second half of your life, which is a boatload of time, and now you know better than to believe someone who spouts off like they know what is best for you.

Think about all of the tech developers over the years who were told no, were rejected, and had doors closed in their faces. Yet they pushed forward and worked out of their garages or parents' houses because they didn't listen to their creativity killers. I would like to take a moment to thank all of the creative geniuses who packed so much goodness and wonder into my iPhone. Holy smoke and pass the gravy, I absolutely love the apps on my phone! I can take a photo of any bush, flower, or tree, and bingo, I can find out what it is and the whole enchilada about how it grows and its leaves, seeds, lifespan—you name it. The same for birds, insects, and clouds. I can play the harmonica with my phone and translate documents. I can scan stuff, print it, fax it, sign it, and send it. I can move money, make money (the real stuff), lose money (more of the real stuff), get money, and spend money without ever seeing money. Siri and I are friends. Well, sometimes I get pissed at her, but most of the time, we are BFFs. I can make videos and play games and edit my photos with even more apps. I even have the whole Multnomah County library in an app on my phone. Love it. So, there is this whole shebang of creativity. Amazing! Thank you for listening and for living in your kick-ass creative zone.

Think about all of the creativity that has poured out over the last decade. Recently, I was looking for a place to spend a few months to do some serious writing away from distractions. I pulled up Airbnb, another creative endeavor started by a few friends. I found my dream writing location at a price I could easily afford, and the communication and process made it safe and seamless. Uber Eats or DoorDash? Lifesavers during stay-at-home time. Right? I went to the dentist a while back, and this guy had puzzles on the ceiling. An entire ceiling full of word puzzles, find-the-objects puzzles, and probably more, but I was finished with my cleaning so I couldn't get to them all. Talk about creativity oozing off of the ceilings! A friend recently told me that their dentist had *Where's Waldo?* on their ceiling. Ummm...I want to go there.

CREATIVE INVENTIONS

Have you ever traveled to a country where you drive on the opposite side of the road? It's terrifying when you first pull out of the airport parking lot of the rental car company! Well, some rental car company in Ireland had the courtesy to put on a dashboard sticker that reflects in the windshield to remind you what side of the road to drive on, so you don't have to wonder. Thank you very much for your kick-ass creativity!

Have you ever seen the elevator buttons you can press with your feet when your hands are full? Who wouldn't love those? Kudos to the creative geniuses who thought that up. Creative problem solving and thinking—gotta love it!

I don't know about you, but I feel like crap when I see dead animals on the side of the road. I recently read about places in Canada and the US where they put up high fences in areas where animals cross and funnel the animals either over or under the highways. I saw this recently in Florida in the habitat of the endangered Florida panther. Creative. Problem. Solvinggggg. These people were observant and figured out a way to reduce the number of animal deaths on the highway. Brilliant and kick-ass, yet again!

Sometimes, with a work group, an individual, or maybe even people at a family gathering, you may ask, "What can I do about xyz?" or "How could we go about fixing abc?" I've said that very thing when driving across the US and seeing acres and acres of wind turbines standing strong on the hillsides just waiting for a breeze or wind to swing by and make them dance. But that dance kills so many birds, and even though I am for alternate energy sources, I have to wonder: at what cost? Then, lo and behold, I read about a company in Spain called Vortex Bladeless that is designing wind turbines with no blades. What the hell? No blades? That got my attention fast, and I found out that the rather phallic-looking machines swaying from side to side get energy from the wind through oscillation, without blades, gears, oil, or brakes. The company will be making small ones for small areas like homes or farms. Wowzers. I love this stuff!

One of the reasons I enjoy traveling to remote places so much is that I get to see creative solutions in action and the benefits they bring to people in rural and remote places.

A friend brought an organization called the Borgen Project to my attention. They work "to raise public and political awareness of ways that life can be improved for people who are struggling to survive." Below are some of the projects they are promoting.

- The Tiger Toilet Sanitation System made an impact on me based on its name alone, as it brought up images of tigers down in pits, but the reality is that 4 billion people in the world still do not have access to safe and dependable sanitation. This system uses no water, so it doesn't rely on septic tanks or water treatment plants. It uses tiger worms, which are usually found around cattle, to clean up the poop. The tiger worms are happy in the pit, changing the waste into water and compost without any smell. This system is being used in rural and poor areas in India with great success and is expanding to other places in the world too.

- RoughRider Wheelchairs, made by Whirlwind Wheelchair, is helping the over 20 million people in developing countries who are in need of a wheelchair. The company has been in business over thirty years, has factories in sixty countries, and works tirelessly to change public policy for people with disabilities. The RoughRider Wheelchair has fifteen different seat settings, is extremely durable, and can handle all kinds of terrain. It is affordable, portable, and easy to repair—all things that are necessary for the people who need them. I see people in wheelchairs and have spent time with them in the past, but I never really thought about how difficult it might be to navigate uneven ground, rocks, and dips and gullies. It is great to know there are chairs that can accommodate those terrains.

- The Hippo Roller was invented by Pettie Pelzer and Johan Jonker, two South Africans who real-

ized there had to be a better and easier way for the
thousands of children and older women who spent
hours each day going back and forth to the nearest
well to fill up their containers. They figured out a
simple, affordable way for those same people to
bring back ninety liters (twenty-four gallons) at a
time rather than a few liters in a small container.
The durable plastic container, which looks like
a hippo body, can be pushed along bumpy roads
and through fields, sand, and all manner of terrain
and has handles attached on the ends for balance.
Rolling it looks like pushing a round suitcase. Since
their invention in 1991, sixty thousand Hippo Roll-
ers have been put into use in fifty-one countries
and have helped more than 600,000 people, with
more benefiting every day. Just this one invention
freed up many hours a day for young girls who can
now dedicate that time to education. The water
they transport is being used to irrigate gardens and
ensure hygiene is part of daily life.

It doesn't take rocket science to make a big difference in
people's lives. Shall I say it again? It takes creative thinking
and problem solving and, yes, getting the hell out of your
comfort zone.

Another water-related invention (can you tell I have a passion
for good water for everyone?) is the LifeSaver Cube.

- The LifeSaver Cube stores up to five liters of water
  and gives a family of four safe daily drinking water
  for a whole year. This product is used for human-
  itarian needs, from victims of natural disasters

to groups of people displaced by war and other conflicts. These products, with cartridges capable of filtering thousands of liters of water, come in all sizes, are portable and durable, and have also become popular with campers, backpackers, and all manner of explorers. I have had one of the individual bottles for several years and it still works great. One of the Cubes should be part of everyone's emergency supplies. Seriously, what would we do, how would we live, if people didn't step out of their comfort zones and own the crap out of their creative minds! Step into yours; seriously, you can be a world changer!

Food and clean water are essential to maintaining good health, but it has to start when children are born. One device that stands out is a newborn phototherapy unit called Firefly. The designers at Design That Matters, a nonprofit, created Firefly to treat infants with jaundice in low-resource hospitals in Asia, Africa, and the Caribbean. This ingenious company designed a product that was difficult to use incorrectly. It fits one infant instead of many, which reduces the risk of infection. It is simple to clean because the rounded bassinet has no seams, and it shines light from above as well as below, which reduces treatment time. It is energy-efficient, using just thirty watts. It is easy to move, small, and durable, so it can be used in the mother's recovery room, and it is functional for five years of twenty-four/seven use. The LEDs last up to forty-four thousand hours. Partners, healthcare workers, corporate sponsors, international aid groups, and government agencies work together to make sure things run smoothly and continue to reach out to more hospitals in more countries where the unit could make a positive impact.

You can see that there are wonderful inventions helping people. And there are other people dedicated to making sure the oceans are protected.

The oceans have become the dumping ground for shipping companies, factories, and our own plastic waste for way too long. Right now, in the Pacific Ocean between Hawaii and California is the largest of five plastic accumulation zones in the world. That one is currently twice the size of Texas and three times the size of France and is getting bigger all the time. That is a shit ton of crap that we dumped. But hey, we do like those single-use water bottles, and Coca Cola makes sure they are easy to get. But many people feel that if they don't have to see it, then it doesn't exist. Well, it doesn't work that way. The rivers and oceans and everything that lives in them or near them is suffering, and that filters down to us too, impacting our ecosystems, health, and economies.

One group dear to my heart that I want you to know about is the Ocean Cleanup. As they say on their website, "The Ocean Cleanup is a nonprofit organization developing advanced technologies to rid the oceans of plastic." They are working on cutting off the source of the plastic and cleaning up the accumulation. They have identified one thousand rivers around the world that push about 80 percent of the plastic into the oceans, so they are working to stop this plastic at its source so it never even reaches the oceans. Concurrently, they are using scientific methods to capture the large and small plastic particles already floating around in the oceans and in these huge "garbage patches." Their creative staff is from all over the world, and they talk about not only their successes but also their failures and how to turn these into workable solutions. This is an amazing group of people doing incredible work that will benefit not only us but all future generations.

Rarely do just one or two people create something that makes life easier for others. We might be aware of one or two names that are involved, but there are countless others making it all happen.

I'm going to close out this chapter now with a wonderful creative story I heard on a creativity podcast called *Spark and Fire*. There are a lot of creativity podcasts out there, but this one touches my heart and speaks to me the most about what the essence of creativity really is.

Bill T. Jones, now sixty-four and an amazing dancer, choreographer, and visionary, along with his collaborator and associate artistic director, Janet Wong, were getting ready to bring out a new work that they and the dancers had been working on for a long time, but then the whole country got gut punched with COVID in early 2020 and their lives as they knew them took a big hit. All seemed lost. New York City was emptying out, and Bill didn't know when he would see his dancers again. Even though his big dream had to be put on hold, he felt a responsibility to his dancers, to keep them employed and to make sure their lives were stable.

When faced with the crisis of how to move forward, Janet Wong knew a way. Instead of going forward, they decided to go backwards. Bill had many old videos of things he had done with his partner, Arnie Zane, before Arnie died of AIDS. But these were things from the 1980s. Bill wasn't sure. Bill and Janet set up weekly Zoom meetings with the dancers. They went into the archives and dug out old "phrases." A phrase is a series of movements linked together. These phrases could be manipulated any way the dancers wanted. Even though the dancers were used to working together, now they worked in their living rooms, rooftops, fields, parks, or wherever they could. They would film themselves and then get together on Zoom and watch. Out of this, they saw a new work emerging that reflected this moment in time.

Then things took a turn for the worse. In May 2020, George Floyd was murdered, and a whole other series of issues were pushed into Bill's reality and his sense of what was important. His dancers questioned whether rehearsals should go on when the world was exploding into anger over the continued police brutality against Black people. One of the dancers, Chanel Howard, challenged Bill and his insistence that rehearsals go on. But he listened, and her words helped the company move into the crisis with a deeper understanding of and commitment to what they needed and wanted to be doing as a group. Bill's worry deepened, and then, out of the blue, they were offered a commission for a socially distanced piece by Michael Lonergan, producer at the Park Avenue Armory. Wow. Could they do it? Bill said yes, they could do it if Michael would give them ten days in the space. And they did.

In the huge Armory space, there were seats for only one hundred people, eleven feet apart. There was tape on the floor where the dancers could perform, and even though the company is known for their partnering, the dancers could not touch or hold hands or be close enough to breathe on each other. They made it work. The performance was truly amazing on many levels and greatly appreciated by all. They found a new kind of creativity that mirrored what people were feeling and thinking and deeply moved the audience.

Janet Wong summed it up with these words: "I always think that obstacles and limitations just allow us to think differently and create things that you would never create under normal circumstances." These are just a few of many examples of putting creativity into action to make life easier for people and animals. Maybe these will spark some creative juices in you too. Creativity is something you have, are capable of doing, and that you do for love. It is about discovering the truth within you and what you are capable of, the things that make you feel at your most authentic, and if you haven't noticed, creativity is essential to personal fulfillment.

After all is said and done, I want to throw another creative idea at you. How about creativity as ideas having sex? Fun, experimental, outrageous, dangerous, exhilarating, exhausting, sometimes good, other times not so much, enjoyable, and satisfying. The origin of ideas having sex came from Matt Ridley, author of *How Innovation Works*, talking about some of the first coffee houses where people came together to discuss ideas. But hey, it works here too. Go ahead and let those ideas have lots of sex—hanging-from-the-chandeliers sex. After your ideas multiply like bunnies, we're going to start changing our lives through the lens of our mindset.

YOUR KICK-ASS MANTRA

"My creativity is kick-ass and brilliant!"

Chapter 7

MINDSET, LOOKING THE WORLD STRAIGHT IN THE EYE!

The ability to wade through the shit-ton of self-doubt and fear that covers us in darkness can happen with mindset. Just wanting to do something doesn't cut it for very long. Graveyards are full of good intentions and broken dreams.

What we need is a way to automate what we do to get through the bad times (and even the good). We need to develop habits, systems, and procedures that shield us from everything life throws at us. If you are like me, that has been a boatload of indecision, procrastination, and doubt for many years. No more time for that. We need to get tough, stay tough, and bring others with us.

What is mindset, and what effects can it have?

I first learned about the word "mindset" in 2006 when I read Carol Dweck's book *Mindset: The New Psychology of Success.* I had just gotten my master's in education and one of my professors recommended it to me. According to Dweck, "a mindset is **a self-perception or 'self-theory' that people hold about themselves**." She feels that "the hand you are dealt is just the starting point for development."

However, many people believe that ability is fixed, something you are born with and you cannot change. You either have it or you don't. That is called a fixed mindset.

On the other hand, if you feel you can develop your ability through hard work and effort, then you have a growth mindset. Carol Dweck's book focuses on students and how they are educated and encouraged at home and in the educational system—and why this is the best time and place to start the growth mindset process. The amazing thing is that it isn't just children who have these mindsets; it works basically the same with people who are older.

After getting my master's and thinking of the students I'd taught over the years, I found that much of what she said was right on. And I wanted to experiment further.

HOW DOES THE CONCEPT OF "MINDSET" WORK?

When I went into the Peace Corps in 2008, I was teaching at a university in Ukraine with students who were the first generation to be out from under Soviet rule. I wondered if the concept of mindset worked there too. In Ukraine, at that time, students came into the university when they were sixteen or seventeen years old but attended for five years.

The strange part to me was that the students were placed in groups based on test scores and other things I wasn't aware of, and for five years, they stayed with and had every class with that same group. No chance to mingle or get to know other students or advance to another group.

It became clear to me that this system was flawed from the get-go, because I had students in my "lowest level" who tried harder and were better students than those in my upper levels. It took me a hell of a long time to figure out a way around that. These students had a classic case of growth mindset, and I wasn't about to let them flounder around and not reach the success they deserved.

I've never been a big fan of "rules" and felt they were more like guidelines than something to be rigidly adhered to. I mean, if you are in the middle of a desert and come to a stop sign, and you can see twenty miles in each direction and no one is coming, will you be slamming on your brakes or looking left and right and cruising on through?

So these "rules" that the students had to stay with their group even though they were way beyond most of the other students didn't sit right with me. Damn, I see I've gotten off track. The bottom line is that I dug into the ministry of education and looked at all of the paperwork and what was required to move forward, how that was evaluated, and so on, and I damn well moved a bunch of students around.

My point is that I could see this mindset theory at work in first-through fifth-year students, and even the professors. To tell you the truth, after I left Ukraine and went on to other things in my life, I didn't think about it again until a few years later when I was involved with conflict resolution and mediation and working with adults and juveniles through a court system. In fact, I can see different mindsets at work whenever I'm around people.

FIXED MINDSET

Growing up poor, I had a fixed mindset. My father only got as far as the eighth grade and my mother got her GED in her fifties. There weren't a lot of books in the house, and I was never encouraged or got help with homework. I worked in the berry and bean fields growing up and got my first job at fifteen. It was expected that I would take care of myself after that. I had this idea that being poor was just the way it was. That was my mindset at the time.

I don't think you can erase many years of the wrong kind of advice in a short time. There are good reasons why we find it hard to stick to good habits or try new things, but most of the time, the challenge is in our head. That little niggling voice that doesn't shut up. We know our mind is a powerful thing.

The things that we tell ourselves and that we actually believe can either help us grow or prevent us from seeing possibilities. If you believe certain limiting things about yourself, it will be difficult for you to get going. A few quick examples:

"I'm not good with numbers."

"I'm not creative."

"I'm not good with tech stuff."

"I can't grow anything."

"I'm always procrastinating."

"I just can't lose weight."

"I can't get motivated to exercise."

"I don't know what to write about."

These fixed mindsets will keep you from doing anything that might cause you to feel like a failure. Fixed-mindset people see failure and rejection as negative things rather than as opportunities for something different.

What are some other fixed-mindset examples that we all buy into from time to time? And how should we respond to those?

You: I could never do that.

Me: This is a great place to start, as we have probably all thought it from time to time. But if we have never tried something, how can we possibly know if we could do it or not? I usually say things like "I could never do that" when something scares the crap out of me. But what if I were able to look at that fear a bit more rationally and see if there was a way? Could you do that too?

You: It's too late to learn that new tech stuff.

Me: Well, you damn well know that it is never too late to learn something, and the day we stop learning is the day we stop living. With all of the online information and free resources out there, we can learn anything.

You: I'll probably just fail, so why even try?

Me: Yep, you might fail a bunch of times. Stop thinking of failure like something that happened to you when you were a child, such as losing a game, getting a bad grade, or falling off your bike a bunch of times. The idea that those were negative things was drummed into you, but failure doesn't equal negative or bad or worthless or anything like that. Think of failure as a reason and an opportunity to look at the situation with new eyes.

A lot of fixed-mindset people assume that their intelligence, creativity, personality, and characteristics cannot be changed and that what they were born with is what they have available. They constantly strive for success and avoid failure or blame it on others because they fear what other people will think of them.

GROWTH MINDSET

If you talk to many authors, you will definitely run into people who are used to rejection.

Robert Pirsig, who wrote *Zen and the Art of Motorcycle Maintenance*, was rejected 121 times even though his editor said, "The book is brilliant beyond belief. It is probably a work of genius and will, I wager, attain classic status." And it did. The book sold millions of copies.

Jack Canfield and Mark Victor Hansen had a similar experience, but they received 144 rejections from publishers. Well, *Chicken Soup for the Soul* became a best seller, then a series, and now a multi-armed franchise. Canfield says, "If we had given up after 100 publishers, I likely would not be where I am now. I encourage you to reject rejection. If someone says no, just say NEXT." I have put the words "next" and "yet" on a sticky note on my laptop to look at when I get frustrated and want to give up.

Eventually, my own mindset began shifting as I grew up. I got some of this from my teachers, who could see my potential where it was shielded from me. My grandmother was also a big influence on shifting my mindset, and I still remember her lessons today.

I've been challenging what it means to get older since I was sixty and decided I was going to do it my way and to hell with the "rules" society had dumped on us as we aged. What a load of crap. What became clear to me when I examined how I looked at things was that I often had a fixed mindset and probably, overall, a combination of fixed and growth.

I ran into a group of diverse personalities at an entrepreneur workshop I attended in Las Vegas who were all growth-mindset inventors. I felt like I was with a bunch of kids with gray hair and a few wrinkles. They were waving their arms around, scribbling on paper, smiling and laughing, and having a great time. I got energized just hanging out with them.

I've invented new ways of doing things and am always looking for shortcuts and more efficiency, but I really admire people who invent things you can pick up and use. Often, that old TV show *MacGyver* pops into my head when I am using a paper clip to fish out something from a drain or as a zipper pull-up.

According to an article in the *New York Times,* there are groups of older inventors out there firing up their imaginations and creativity and coming up with some amazing inventions. Since becoming a minimalist, I've also become very creative in using what I have in multiple different ways. Right now, I have a favorite glass that I use as a drinking water glass, coffee cup, wine glass, vase, measuring cup, and even a bug catcher.

Constance Gustke's article in the *New York Times* quotes several members of inventing communities who pretty much sum up what's going on in that world. John Calvert, past executive director of the United Inventors Association said, "There's a boom in inventions by people over 50." Over 60 percent of the association's members are older, he added, so they also have more time for inventing. Louis J. Foreman, founder of Edison Nation, noted that people over fifty are more educated, active, and mobile, which helps them invent solutions to problems that older people deal with every day.

It seems that an active imagination is more important than a vast warehouse of knowledge when it comes to inventing. Warren Tuttle, also from the United Inventors Association, added that inventors include people who drop out of high school and others who are PhDs. He noted that women inventors are especially creative because they recognize the benefit of a product and reverse engineer how to make it.

Mr. Tuttle also felt that older inventors can better focus on a project and went on to say, "When some people meet rejections they give up. So, you need lots of stick-to-itiveness." I can relate to this a lot as I have family members who give up after trying something once. They make up a lot of stuff in their head about why it might not work, or they make one or two mistakes and don't find what it takes to go forward. I think living life and getting to where we are in life has given us a lot of tools we aren't even aware of.

Dr. Gary Small, professor of psychiatry and director of the UCLA Longevity Center, said, "Short-term memory does decline but people become more empathetic as they get older. And this is an essential ingredient in creating products for others." He went on to say, "Lifelong learning also lowers the risk for dementia. People who are great inventors observe the world and take it in."

Those with a growth mindset look at failure as a challenge and an opportunity to learn. They build on their abilities. They know that it takes time and effort to reach success, but the process of getting there is just as important as reaching the goal. They know that practice and learning lead to the high level of achievement they want.

A GROWTH MINDSET OVERTURNS MANDATORY RETIREMENT

Maggie Kuhn started the Gray Panthers movement in 1970 when she was sixty-five years old. She had been an activist for most of her life and cared for her mother, who needed assistance due to a disability, and a brother with mental illness. She worked on behalf of global peace, human rights, social and economic justice for underprivileged people, and integration.

She became interested in elder rights in 1961 when she attended a White House conference on aging. She led a protest of over one thousand around the White House, demanding they be included in the conference. She was forced to retire from a job she loved, working for the Presbyterian church, and that set her on fire. Although her employer loved her too, at that time, people were forced to retire at age sixty-five.

This led to her forming the Gray Panthers with a bunch of people she knew who had also been forced to retire. Many others in the movement were in high school and college, and their motto was "Age and Youth in Action." Maggie felt society should take younger people more seriously and give them more responsibility.

The Gray Panthers lobbied against mandatory retirement. Congress raised the age to seventy in 1978 and then eliminated it altogether in 1986. Some industries still maintain a retirement age, like the airline industry, where the retirement age is sixty. That seems reasonable for safety reasons, but perhaps that will change too as people live healthier and longer lives.

There are lots of horror stories out there about people who were just let go and never had a proper retirement send-off, even after many years of working for a company. But that isn't always so, and I had the opportunity to witness a lovely retirement by a United Airlines pilot.

A few years ago, I was returning from Australia, which is probably the longest flight I have taken at one go. I had paid extra to have more room and comfort, but when I got to the airport in Sydney, it was crammed with people sleeping all over the place, looking exhausted.

I found out there had been a very bad storm, many flights had been canceled, and some people had been there more than two days. Consequently, my nice seat with the extra room and comfort was no longer available, and I now had a seat in the middle of a row of five. I gave myself ten seconds to be a whiny bitch and then was just thankful I could get on the plane.

I think those long flights have a huge staff to take care of everyone, as I must have seen ten wandering around in my section alone. They were all wearing buttons with a guy's face on them. Being the curious person that I am, I asked one of them what the deal was with the guy on the button. "Oh, he is our main pilot, and this is his last flight. We love him and will miss him terribly, so we are having this little party for him. His wife is in first class, and he doesn't know it. Yet." Big smiles.

So, we are flying into the San Francisco airport, coming in low over the water, and on either side of the runway were what seemed like hundreds of fire trucks with their hoses shooting water up into the air in a huge arc, which the plane came down into. We had been told this was going to happen and it wasn't an emergency, so no one was worried.

It felt like their version of an honor guard doing a twenty-one-gun salute. We all cheered, and suddenly the flight took on a different meaning. I was so glad I had the opportunity to experience what a good retirement could look like. But truthfully, I'm not sure the word "retirement" is valid anymore. It doesn't exist in many cultures, and maybe we need to let it go extinct.

We know Maggie Kuhn didn't buy into retirement and, in fact, used it to springboard into making changes that benefited all of us. She certainly had a growth mindset that was open to all kinds of possibilities.

NUMEROUS POSSIBILITIES OPEN
WHEN "RETIREMENT" IS OBSOLETE

Consider Arnold Schwarzenegger, who didn't buy into retirement and became governor of California in his sixties. Or Teiichi Igarashi, a former lumberjack who, at age eighty-nine, decided to climb Mount Fuji and climbed every year until he was one hundred. And you probably know of Frank McCourt, who wrote *Angela's Ashes* but didn't start writing until he was sixty-five. None of them bought into "retirement," and they couldn't have accomplished what they did without an open mind and a growth mindset.

Another fun story that I love to tell is about a runner from Australia. At sixty-one years old, Cliff Young entered to run the extremely difficult Sydney to Melbourne ultramarathon. This is a 543.7 mile (875 km to the rest of the world) endurance race that takes up to five days.

Cliff showed up in his overalls and work boots. The rest of the runners were generally under thirty years old and at the top of their game, with sponsors like Nike. They had been preparing hard. And damn, they looked good in their flashy outfits and running shoes.

The race organizers were very skeptical, but Cliff assured them he could do it. The press also gave him a hard time with teasing. Cliff told them that, as a kid, he was dirt poor and lived on a farm of about 2,000 acres (809.37 hectares) and his family had 2,000 sheep. If a storm was coming, Cliff would be sent out to round up the sheep and bring them in. They were in a depression and very poor. They had no machinery or horses, but they did have

Cliff. Sometimes it would take him three days to round them all up, but he did it. In his galoshes. He could do this.

When the race started, people were in disbelief. This guy was way too old to do this run, he didn't have on brand-name shoes, he wasn't wearing any logo-enhanced clothing, and he looked way too happy. Off they went, with dust blowing in Cliff's face as he watched the other runners slowly get smaller and smaller.

The people along the route and the press were curious; they were intrigued by this guy. He didn't even seem to run properly. He had this slow, shuffling kind of run going on. Now, normally, to finish this difficult long-distance run, the competitors would run for eighteen hours and then rest for six. But Cliff didn't know this, so he passed the other runners while they were sleeping the first night and kept on shuffling along.

The next day, the runners passed him again and they were really surprised to see him still in the race. The crowd and the press were loving this—it was like the tortoise and the hare. Cliff's plan was to continue running until the end of the race. He kept narrowing the gap, and by the last night, his slow shuffle had moved him to the head of the pack. Cliff ended up winning the race ten hours ahead of the next person and, of course, he set a new race record.

There was a $10,000 prize (which would be over $35,000 today) but Cliff didn't even know there was a prize, and he felt the other runners had worked just as hard as he had, so he didn't keep any for himself and shared it with the other competitors. He ran the race several more times and became a legend while raising money for homeless kids. Several ultramarathon runners now use his shuffle and don't sleep at night.

With his growth mindset, he took on something he had never done before, tested the limits of his physical and mental endurance, and changed a lot of minds about who can run and how long they can do it. Cliff definitely didn't care what other people thought because he knew differently, and that is what was important to him.

Clara McBride Hale was an amazing woman. Her father was killed when she was young and then her mother died when she was sixteen, leaving Clara an orphan. She finished high school on her own and then married Thomas Hale. They moved to New York City and had three children.

Things were going well, but then Thomas died of cancer. Clara cleaned houses and was a janitor, but that didn't give her enough time with her children, so she opened her home for day care and night care, as many mothers had to work all night. The children she cared for became very attached to her and soaked up the love and encouragement she gave them. Her children thought of them as siblings. She provided a great service to her neighborhood in New York City.

In 1940, she received a license to take foster children into her home. She raised forty children who were loved, treated with respect, had a lot of self-esteem, and went into the world feeling good about themselves. She provided foster care for over twenty-five years and retired in 1968, when she was sixty-four.

But she wasn't finished yet. In 1969, her daughter brought her a mother and young baby who were in fragile health and in trouble. While Mrs. Hale was making a phone call, the woman left and abandoned her baby, who was suffering from drug withdrawal. Mrs. Hale nursed the child through that trauma, and within weeks, word had spread and her apartment was filled with drug-addicted babies.

Mrs. Hale and her children worked day and night to help these babies. Her children had a slew of jobs to make money to support all of the children. Soon, all of this help and caring was noticed by agencies, bureaus, and people who wanted to give some assistance. The Hales got a grant to fix up a great old five-story house on 122nd Street and had additional help from Percy Sutton, a philanthropist, and John Lennon, who donated a large amount of money. Many others donated, too, when they found out what great work she was doing.

In 1986, it was estimated that over five hundred babies and toddlers had been rescued from drug addiction and the pain and loneliness of AIDS (which the children were infected with through their mothers). But Clara also helped the parents with counseling, finding housing, and other needs. In 1989, after twenty years of giving service, only twelve children had to be put up for adoption. The others were returned to their families.

Clara McBride Hale received many honors and spoke about her work all over the United States. She was honored by President Ronald Reagan at his State of the Union address and sat next to Nancy Reagan on the stage. In 1989, she received the Harry S. Truman Public Service Award.

She was always humble wherever she went, and it was clear that all she really cared about were the babies and making sure they were safe and healthy. She famously said, "Help one another. Love each other." She is a wonderful example of living a growth mindset and finding ways to continue to make things work even when they seem impossible.

CHANGE YOUR MINDSET, CHANGE YOUR LIFE

Are there ways to change your mindset from fixed to growth? All I can say for sure is that it worked for me, and I am confident it will work for you too. Here are a few of the ways you can change your beliefs.

Don't stop learning. Learning doesn't stop when you reach a certain age. Learning new things, doing new things, and even thinking about new things creates new neural pathways. And with the things you already know, lots of new ideas and possibilities start to fall in place.

Embrace failure. Failure is a good time to learn something. If you are going to have a growth mindset, then you will learn how to fail with a purpose because learning from your mistakes is what moves you toward success.

Embrace constructive criticism. Listen to what people are telling you about what you are doing. Get out your sieve and let the crap and negative stuff drop away, but hang on to the constructive criticism. That kind of feedback is gold. And you will know the difference right away.

Learn perseverance. Try, try again. As adults, we somehow feel we should be able to do something new the first time we try it. Well, think again. A growth mindset reminds you that the more effort and practice you put into something, the better you will be.

Learn from others. Stand on the shoulders of giants. Look to the people you admire and appreciate and learn from them, whether they are in a field you are interested in or something else. What can you learn from these people? Don't try to reinvent the wheel. Model others and learn their skills.

Ask what else you could do. If something doesn't work out the way you want it to, ask yourself how you could do things differently next time. Whether it is a meeting or a new recipe or planning a vacation, it is just fine to critique what you did, what worked, and what you could do differently or better the next go around.

Start where you are. When you have a growth mindset, you know that you have to start where you are with each new skill that you learn. Will the learning curve be steep? Maybe so, but you will be ready.

Embrace challenges. Challenges build mental muscles. You've had a lifetime of difficult choices to make so far in your life, and they have made an impact on who you are as a person. Each new challenge is an opportunity to gain experience and grow as a role model for others.

Have confidence. Believing in yourself makes you the captain of your ship. You are more likely to know how to avoid the rocks and stick with your course even if a storm blows you around.

Embrace the power of Y-E-T. Don't let anyone or anything stop you from doing what you want to do. And most of all, don't stop yourself. Remember, when you can't do something the first time or the hundredth time, just say, "I am unable to do it YET."

Ignore the detractors. The niggling voice that never shuts up isn't who you are. It is a voice from when people lived with the danger of being eaten by a tiger or falling off a cliff. Tell the voice you are fine and will make sure to let it know if you need help. Otherwise, tell it to STFU (shut the fuck up).

If you can visually step outside of yourself to look at your voice and see it separate from who you are, it will change your world. When you do this, you can look your voice, yourself, and the world straight in the eye and with a growth mindset. Then you can live the kick-ass life you know, deep down, that you deserve and want. But I'll tell you something I've learned: you can't get there without motivation. Let's explore that in the next chapter. Get hungry for a big motivation sandwich!

YOUR KICK-ASS MANTRA

"I will have a kick-ass second half of my life, because it is my choice."

Chapter 8

MOTIVATION

Are You Hungry?

Let me begin this chapter with a few "must dos" for a kick-ass way of living.

1. Level up your patience and be good to yourself. Take it a bit at a time for yourself.

2. Pick and choose. Some things you will already be doing and others you most likely won't or shouldn't give a rat's ass about. Let's look at intrinsic and extrinsic motivation first.

INTRINSIC VERSUS EXTRINSIC MOTIVATION

The findings of Edward Deci and Richard Ryan, who wrote *Self Determination Theory: Basic Psychological Needs in Motivation, Development, and Wellness*, demonstrate motivation very well.

The authors found a distinction between controlled motivation, where you are seduced or pressured into doing something and you have to do it, and autonomous motivation, which means it is your choice to do what you are doing.

You have most likely heard about intrinsic and extrinsic motivation. Fun words to roll around in your mouth, but they more or less mean stuff you do because you want to and think it would be a good thing to do versus stuff you do because you get some money, a raise, or a gold watch or someone tells you that you have to do it. Deci and Ryan challenged the idea that a person either had the right amount of motivation for a certain job or they didn't. They thought there might be different types of motivation that produced different results. So, through many experiments and much analysis, they compared intrinsic drivers, like passion, against extrinsic drivers, like prestige.

They found out that intrinsic motivation or drive is much more effective than extrinsic motivation. To clarify, basic needs such as food, shelter, and safety have to be met first, as shown in Maslow's hierarchy. When those needs are met, the other motivators can kick in. They went on to discover that doing what you want to be doing (autonomous motivation) supersedes being pressured into doing something (controlled motivation). No surprise there if you look at what really motivates you. The authors found that people who were doing something because they felt they had to often ended up taking shortcuts. When they were doing what they did because of interest, enjoyment, and the fact that it lined up with their values, autonomous motivation was working. It seems autonomy turns us into a much more effective version of ourselves. When we are in the driver's seat, we're more focused, productive, optimistic, creative, and healthy.

DAGWOOD SANDWICHES

Now that we know those different types of motivation, we can look at all the things that make up the various parts we have to work with. These ingredients remind me of a Dagwood sandwich. If you aren't familiar with this type of sandwich or you haven't stopped to google it yet, a Dagwood is a tall sandwich made with a variety of meats, cheeses, and condiments. Many different layers, much like life, and it's a huge sandwich. Think really, really big! I like to break down how motivation works using this delicious sandwich as a reference point. I do this in my own life. Yep! I live a Dagwood-sandwich kind of life.

Motivation

Visualize motivation like the bread. The very first layer of a sandwich is the most important. It is the foundation. It is important to add the layers in order as we build the motivation masterpiece. Autonomy, curiosity, passion, massive transformative purpose, high hard goals, and finally clear goals.

Autonomy

Then you can add autonomy. Autonomy is self-governance, where you decide how, when, and where you will do the projects and achieve your goals. This is especially important in the second half of life because many people did not have autonomy during their working years. They satisfied the goals of their employers, but they got left behind.

Autonomy is also an important ingredient in the motivation mix because it reduces stress while increasing satisfaction, well-being, and creativity.

Everyone reading this can own that they have the ability to make their own decisions at every single level, and to do this, they will need to be on top of their motivation. We are 100 percent responsible for our own lives and our own decisions, and we will need constant motivation to stay in check.

Curiosity

Now that we are able to do what we want, when we want and how we want to, it's time to get really curious about just what it is we might want to learn more about. Being curious about something gets the brain working and excited.

Curiosity is one of my favorite things about living a kick-ass second half of my life, and it is one of the things I like most about myself. I was born curious. I'm just curious as hell about most everything. Nature, for sure, why humans do what they do, how things work or don't work, and the universe... You get the picture. But here's the thing: curiosity has opened many doors for me. Actually, being an introvert most of the time, I am surprised I am willing to go out of my way to talk to someone because I am curious about something. I think it has to do with a quick relationship that doesn't demand too much of me. Curiosity definitely overrides my introverted nature.

THOUGHT EXERCISE / ACTION STEP

Grab a pen and paper. Yes, yet again. It is one of the most effective ways to get things done and to help you remember. You can use sticky notes or index cards. Write down ten to twenty-five things you are curious about. You will need to broaden your curiosity scope beyond things like "I'm curious about the weather this weekend" or "I wonder what to serve those twenty people coming for dinner on Saturday."

Curious in this sense means if you had a weekend or two to read a couple of books, watch a program, or talk with someone who is an expert in a particular field, who, where, and what would this be? More than just a passing inquiry, this is something that grabs your attention. It is motivational energy.

You are looking for new and challenging topics, topics that you want to and can become fully absorbed in, to the point where you are willing to devote time and thought to answer some of your questions. You will need this kind of energy to push away distractions that want to buzz in your ear like that nighttime mosquito.

There will be eight more action steps in this chapter, so get ready.

When I went to write down the twenty-five things I was curious about, it took me a week. I bottomed out at four the first time. I had to walk away and think about it. I realized I had shut off my childlike excitement and my desire to explore with abandon and had become way too uptight about what I thought I should be spending my time on.

My beginner's mind was snoozing away in the basement of childhood dreams. Yes, I was curious, but was I curious enough to spend a weekend researching, reading, and talking to people about a topic? That was the question that kept coming back to me. So take your time with this step too, as curiosity is one of the basic ingredients of passion.

According to *New York Times* bestselling author Steven Kotler, when we leverage curiosity to look for our passions, we trigger two vital mental skills: the desire to search out novel and challenging situations and the ability to become fully absorbed in these interesting situations. This helps you increase the motivational energy necessary to train up the state of consciousness required to stay in the game for as long as it takes.

THOUGHT EXERCISE / ACTION STEP

You are going to want to visualize these twenty-five curiosities, and there are several ways you can do that. I have used sticky notes and index cards, but pieces of paper will do fine, or making two columns on a piece of paper with your curiosities on one side will work as well.

If you are using sticky notes, get yourself a big piece of paper or use your dining room table. Think big. Draw (or visualize) a circle large enough so that you can place these twenty-five sticky notes (or however many you end up with) around the circle at even intervals. Then number the sticky notes and their location on the paper. If this seems confusing, have a glass of wine and read on. If you are using index cards, just lay them out in rows so you can see everything at one time. The next thing you want to do is hunt for intersections.

THOUGHT EXERCISE / ACTION STEP

Study all of your curiosities and see if they overlap or are in any way related to other things you have written down. If you drew a circle with sticky notes, draw a line from one to the other across the page, up and down, or however they combine. If you are using index cards, pretend you are playing solitaire and stack up those that are similar or are related in some way. You will end up with some that are related and a few that are just hanging out being interesting. Save those. But look at the ones that overlap—that is where you will find energy and possibility.

My main intersections and overlaps are environmental stuff and looking at ways people over fifty or sixty can recreate the second half of their lives and make a difference on the planet. That's where I put my focus.

When you have three or four things coming together, more energy is created; your brain starts to recognize patterns and put things together, and it gets excited and gives you a little squirt of your reward chemical, dopamine. Your brain is a virtual store-house of drugs, and dopamine is one you want to have around. Dopamine helps us when we need to focus and pay attention. This attention and focus make learning easier, and that moves us toward progress and performance. Dopamine also creates a feedback loop because it helps us find more patterns to link the things we already know to the things we are learning. It is one of the feel-good drugs our body stores and it gives us a little reward, and who doesn't like rewards? The more we get, the more we want, and that wanting leads us toward passion. Is dopamine an addiction? I don't know, but if it is, it is a good one.

One of my questions when I did the action step above for the first time a few years back was, "Is there a way for people over sixty to work in groups locally, nationally, and internationally, using their expertise and experience to tackle the world's most difficult problems, such as providing fresh water for everyone, cleaning up the oceans, and ensuring clean energy, education for girls, and healthcare for all?" You know, simple stuff. Another question I had was if there was a way to make synthetic compounds that were the same or better than those found in animal parts like horns, scales, and innards that could be available for a reasonable price and that would stop the poaching of endangered animals.

A while back, I was standing on the beach in the Dominican Republic, watching as the waves crashed ashore, the wind blew the palms, and the sun's rays warmed my skin. I wondered if there was a way to harness that energy for the people who lived there without huge wind turbines or other manmade equipment that would ruin the beauty of the place. Your curiosities will be different from mine, but give it a go.

THOUGHT EXERCISE / ACTION STEP

For the next step, after you have found your top curiosities and stacked them up into balls of energy, it is time to get to know these new ideas. This can take a month, a year, or in my case, multiple years.

Start by spending ten to fifteen minutes a day listening to a podcast or lecture, or watching a TED Talk or other video around your curiosity topics. You can also read articles and books. Feed your curiosities a little bit at a time, and watch as your brain brings things together and starts to see patterns and familiarities.

Your brain loves making connections between what you already know and this new information. What you gain over time is some expertise. You are learning new vocabulary, history, and the language used by experts in your field. You will need this history in order to build the structure of your ideas, a place where you can hang your new facts.

Learning the language of your new subject not only allows you to think about it more deeply but also helps you converse with others about the subject. And that will be important in the next step.

To find out if your ideas are sound or have some benefits you want to share, you will need to talk to people. However, at first, be judicious. Don't talk to just anyone. You want successes. That means not talking to family and friends just yet.

Tippy-toe out there and join an online community that is already exploring your pursuit or join a meet-up of others in your interest community. You can look for a Facebook group that has people in your area of curiosity and see what they are saying. Make a comment or two or ask a few questions.

Find out if there are any workshops or seminars about your topic. You will become more and more comfortable as you gain knowledge, and people will want to speak with you and be interested in what you have to say. They will tell you about things they have found out, and you can build on your expertise that way too.

When you have your ideas more fully developed and can answer a lot of questions and let ignorant comments roll off your back, you could talk with your family and friends about what you are pursuing. When you find yourself doing that, you have shifted from curiosity to passion.

THOUGHT EXERCISE / ACTION STEP

Passion

When you have spent a lot of time on a new subject and are still in love with learning more about it, you have discovered a passion. However, if you spent some time and then got bored, just set that aside and stop spending time on it. You will not be passionate about all of your curiosities. And your passions might change. Nothing wrong with that.

Seriously look at those things you have become passionate about, because now it is time to turn passion into purpose. This is where stuff gets done. This is how it works.

Purpose

Now is the time to harness all of that curiosity work into passion and turn it into purpose. Purpose is where you make a difference. This is one of the most important layers because it will continue to drive you on your journey. Purpose is where you build partnerships with others, start new businesses or nonprofits, and make life better for other people and yourself. Remember that stack of curiosities that got you fired up? You're going to need those for this next part.

THOUGHT EXERCISE / ACTION STEP

You will need to get out another piece of paper or continue working in your notebook.

Write down a list of ten to fifteen massive problems facing the world today that you would like to see solved. These should be things everyone has to deal with: climate change, hunger, homelessness, energy scarcity, environmental degradation. As you did with your curiosity list, try to be as specific as possible. This might require some research too. Most massive problems aren't just one problem, but thousands of smaller problems all lumped together. You will need to know what these are.

THOUGHT EXERCISE / ACTION STEP

When you have this list, look for places where your passions intersect with these huge global problems. That intersection is a place where your passion is a solution to some huge problem. And if not the whole solution, then a portion of it. That is your purpose.

> You could be looking at a great business opportunity, with or without partners, and a way to use your newfound passion to do some serious good in the world. This translates into your massive transformative purpose (MTP).

It is good to remember that the world's biggest problems are often the world's biggest business opportunities. And if you really want to cultivate and feed your passion, you've got to find a way to pay for it.

As Steven Kotler talks about in *The Habit of Ferocity*, money, or the lack of it, causes all kinds of safety and security issues. Money-related fears dump stress hormones into the body, and being creative and motivated become difficult. If you are still having difficulty paying the bills and keeping a roof over your head, it's nearly impossible to pay attention to anything else.

So, knowing that those big hairy problems are also the biggest business opportunities is important because when you find ways to link passion to purpose, and purpose to business, you have discovered a way to solve multiple problems at once.

Goals

Now let's look at the other ingredients in the sandwich. We've turned curiosity into passion and passion into purpose. It's time for some goals. Goals, schmoals, right? Until I figured this out, I put goals in the same category as New Year's resolutions.

Thumbs down. Didn't work, didn't like, didn't care. But listen, as far back as Aristotle, setting goals had a big influence of getting a desired outcome or reaching a target. What has been discovered is that not every goal is the same, not every goal is right for every situation, and sometimes the wrong goal in the wrong situation can stick a big wrench in the production wheel.

Lots of research has been done (check out the studies by Latham and Locke), and it has been proven that setting goals can increase productivity by as much as 25 percent. That's a boat load of extra time if you are working for a company. But we're not doing that. We're figuring out how to make our purpose work for us. When you want a huge increase in motivation and productivity, you need some big goals. Big goals work better than medium-sized goals, small goals, and those ever-pervasive vague goals.

THOUGHT EXERCISE / ACTION STEP

The big targets that we want to get to are called the high hard goals or the big goals. These goals are steps you will take to reach your MTP and may include getting a degree, starting a business, creating a nonprofit, or writing a book. High hard goals help us stay persistent, and they focus our attention. But damn, they are big. They will often feel uncomfortable, but that is how you know you have gone big. Go ahead and write some of these down. As you dive deeper, you will be adding to or subtracting from this list.

THOUGHT EXERCISE / ACTION STEP

In come clear goals. Start writing these down for each of your high hard goals. Clear goals are all of the smaller steps we will take along the way to reach our high hard goals. These goals tell us when and where to put our attention. When our goals are as clear as a mountain lake, our mind doesn't have to wander around, trying to figure out what to do next. It already knows.

Non-important stuff gets filtered out, and action and awareness start to come together as our concentration gets more focused. Sounds good, doesn't it? Are you ready for the tricky part? The emphasis has to be on "clear" and not "goals." Clarity equals certainty, and that's what we want at this point. We need to know what to do and where to focus our attention.

Our day-to-day means breaking tasks down into bite-sized chunks and setting goals accordingly.

My high hard goal of writing this book was chunked down to a clear goal of writing two hundred and fifty words a day. Some days I made it and some days I didn't, but some days I wrote five thousand words. You need to figure out what is challenging yet manageable for each of your goals. You need enough stimulation to keep you interested but not so much stress that you give up. The high hard goals might take years, but the clear goals will get done one minute at a time.

Because of your hard work and persistence, you can move right into your purpose, prepared with all of the tools you need.

INSPIRATION

Now that you have the Dagwood sandwich of motivation, let's look at some inspiring real-life examples of motivation involving people in the second half of their lives.

I was recently listening to an episode of the wonderful podcast *Meditative Story* about Diana Nyad. As an aside, don't let the word "meditative" turn you off, as this is my go-to podcast anytime I am driving through bumper-to-bumper traffic. Oh yes, this is a favorite. Calms me right down. Makes me laser-focused on what needs to happen.

I was interested right away when Diana mentioned a line from a favorite poem, "The Summer Day" by Mary Oliver, and repeated the line "Tell me, what is it you plan to do with your one wild and precious life?" Cuts to the core, huh? You might remember Diana as a world-class long-distance swimmer, but in this episode, she recalled a chance encounter she had with Christopher Reeve after he was paralyzed. At that time, she had been a sports announcer for over twenty years. He was asking her about the essence of her success as a swimmer, and she recalled the last pool race she had competed in. She had told herself, "Every day of your life, no matter what you do, do it so you can't do it a fingernail better. No regrets."

Reeve, strapped in the contraption that held him up, gasping for air that allowed him to get out a few words at a time, a true Superman, stared at her and asked her if she had kept that promise. Her answer was "hardly." Then, a year after her conversation with Reeve at the 2000 Olympics in Sydney, it hit her that she had just become a spectator. Diana was no longer chasing her own dreams but following after others chasing theirs. Later in her office, she found the Mary Oliver poem and recited her favorite line daily throughout the month when she turned sixty. She was ready to get back to "not a fingernail better." She still had one epic adventure she had never forgotten about, even though she failed at it before. She wanted to complete the Mount Everest of the Earth's oceans: the crossing between Havana, Cuba, and Key West, Florida. Think sharks, killer jellyfish, summer storms, and the Gulf Stream, to name a few. The swim is 110.86 miles long, and you don't stop midway for a nice lunch on a yacht.

She attempted the crossing several times, and Mother Nature stomped on her progress. She did another twenty-four-hour swim before bringing things back to Key West and waiting for the weather to clear. Diana recalled being in the water at 2:00 a.m. and knowing the get-out time was 9:00 a.m. She said, "There is no moon. The sea is black. The sky is black. I'm shivering and confused. I'm lost. I'm hanging on by a thread. I'm floundering, nauseous, cold." Her head handler knew she was in trouble and called out to her: "Listen to me! I need to know if you have five more strokes left in you! If you don't, if you can't take five strokes, we're going to pack it up and we can live with that. Do you hear me?" Diana said, in her childlike voice, "I think so."

She pulled it together in what seemed like a Herculean effort and managed five strokes. Then Bonnie, her swimming coach, encouraged her to do five more and then five more, hour after hour, until dawn broke on the horizon. Bonnie knew that seeing the dawn would give Diana hope. And it did. Diana said, "This Cuba Swim is bigger than you and me, Bonnie. Bigger than sports. It's our tribute to living this one wild and precious life." On September 2, 2013, she arrived at Smathers Beach in Key West. She'd swum 110.86 miles in fifty-two hours and fifty-four minutes. Diana knows the whole expedition was about the journey and the life lessons, not the great ending. Now she is stepping up as an activist for the polluted oceans she fell in love with and spent so many hours in, discovering the wonders of living life so well that she couldn't live it a fingernail better.

* * *

Here is another example. Nelson Mandela, as a young lawyer, joined the African National Congress in 1943 and spent his years as a young man fighting for Black rights against apartheid and white minority rule. Mandela was arrested and tried many times, and in 1962, he was imprisoned for conspiring to overthrow the state. He spent twenty-seven years in prison and finally got out in 1990 after international pressure was put on South Africa. In 1964, he said, "I have fought against white domination, and I have fought against black domination. I have cherished the ideal of a democratic and free society in which all persons live together in harmony and with equal opportunities. It is an ideal which I hope to live for and to achieve. But if needs be, it is an ideal for which I am prepared to die." Several years after Mandela's release from prison, when he was seventy-five, he was elected the first Black head of state as president of South Africa in a fully representative democratic election. He clearly achieved his MTP, and even though it took him a very long time, he stayed motivated and encouraged others.

* * *

In 2017, at an awards ceremony for the Breakthrough Foundation's life sciences prize, Joanne Chory, then sixty-three years old, sounded an alarm about climate change, saying that "human-caused climate change was putting humanity's future in peril." She went on to explain what it would take to get rid of greenhouse gases and why there was such an urgency. Not only was she figuring out how to grab hold of climate change and reverse its effects, she was also fighting her own battle with Parkinson's disease, which she was diagnosed with in 2004 when she was only forty-nine years old. Her MTP was "to create ideal plants like wheat and rice that could store huge amounts of carbon in their roots and avoid problems like drought and flooding that takes its toll on the plant material above the ground." Her talk received a lot of attention and funding, and her research went on. She kept working even as the disease she was fighting progressed. In 2016, she and her fellow researchers started working on the Harnessing Plant Initiative.

They developed a plan that included five years of research, five years of field trials, and five years of scaling up production. By 2030, the ideal crops would cover half a million acres. Then by 2035, plants would be able to absorb 10 to 20 percent of current annual emissions. Joanne struggles to stay positive when thinking about a future with "fires, floods, food and water shortages, destruction of habitat, and species extinction," but then sees a future she thinks is possible: "people living in smaller, more sustainable housing, wind and solar power, and farmland planted with engineered crops that are sucking up the carbon dioxide in their deep, strong roots." She is fully aware that her own future is challenging, but she says, "I would like for my kids to be thinking that I did something important for their world." Yes, Joanne, you certainly are doing just that. Thank you.

Now that you've put all the layers of autonomy, curiosity, passion, purpose, MTP, high hard goals, and clear goals into your motivation sandwich, what happens next? Well, a great sandwich wouldn't be complete without a spicy, juicy, crunchy, and satisfying addition like grit, which is akin to a juicy kosher dill pickle. Are you still hungry? Growth seeking and change will make you crave more, eat more, do more, and be more. For that—and anything in life worth doing—we will need grit.

YOUR KICK-ASS MANTRA

"My potential is limitless, and I choose where to spend my energy."

Chapter 9

GRIT

Why It Matters

Holy smoke, here we are at grit already. Let me break it down for you really quickly.

GRIT is an acronym: **G**reatness **R**equires **I**nternal **T**oughness.

This is one of my favorite things to talk about because I see people light up when I explain it. I've seen lives change, including my own, all because the power of grit, once understood, can move mountains.

Angela Duckworth is a psychologist and educator who wrote *Grit: The Power of Passion and Perseverance* in 2016. As an educator, it came to my attention, as I feel the public education system doesn't address what the students need to succeed.

Plus, I was living in Mexico at the time and my grandson had come to live with me down there at age nine, so I was thrust into yet another challenge with learning.

Most of the research for the book was done with students or young adults in college, but I thought a lot of what Duckworth found out was also true for someone like me. Yes, I took Angela Duckworth's Grit Scale quiz on her website, www.angeladuck-worth.com. I think I scored a little over two out of five on the grit scale.

I just took the quiz again while writing this chapter and scored 4.3/5.0. I take it every once in a while, as an indicator of how I feel I am doing with a bunch of things I'm working on. If nothing else, Angela says it is a test for "self-reflection." I see it as an indicator of my mental toughness and how that muscle is developing and staying in shape. For me, it is about making and sticking to daily habits and overcoming challenges and distractions. It is about daily practice and consistency.

Do I do this all the time? Hell no. Sometimes I have gone for months mucking around in the muddy waters of procrastination. But then I get out of the self-absorbed tangle of false crap I have told myself and start again. And I prove to myself that I have the guts to get in the ring, take my punches, and get in a few good ones myself. Those wins feel great.

Then I remember Angela Duckworth's quote: "Grit is living life like it's a marathon not a sprint." And having run a few marathons, I know what she means. Especially the training part.

It takes real guts to keep moving ahead and through all of the piles of negative and messed up stories we tell ourselves when we think the universe and even the people we love are conspiring against us. It takes intention, resilience, and grit to make it through. You wouldn't be here reading this if you didn't have those.

As you will see when you get the test scored on the website, scoring high indicates how much grit you have, given the definition of passion and perseverance. The trick is that she says there are no right or wrong answers. Jeez Louise. How can that be? Well, that's what I thought the first time I took it. I wanted to know if I was "right" or "wrong." What was I supposed to do with this "there are no right or wrong answers"? But the very fact that your score can change is an indication that you can change too, and that's what I did.

I wasn't pleased with the score I got at first, so I implemented the things I have been talking about in the book and put myself on a path to challenge aging, and I haven't looked back. It has been a very bumpy rollercoaster ride, sometimes in the dark, a few times half off the rails, and with huge, steep ups and downs, but I'm still on and don't want to get off.

Look for signs that you have grit, and I'll bet you find them all over the place. Do you have something you spend time on just because you love it? Do you see frustrations as a necessary part of new things you are trying? Do you look for ways to make things easier and more important to you? Do you believe you can change and grow? If you look back over all of the amazing things you have accomplished so far, I think you will see that you are full of grit. One quick way to do that is to look at your life in ten-year chunks to remind yourself of how much you have accomplished and how many difficult times in your life you had to make tough choices and trust yourself. These are all grit indicators.

I am thankful for the test and for all of Angela Duckworth's research and commitment, and I have found that passion and perseverance are right-on-target necessary for the second half of life too, because you will be experiencing different challenges and opportunities that you haven't faced before, and this is where your grit comes into play.

I am also going to share and take the liberty of expanding on a few more types of grit I have found beneficial on this journey into aging and having a boat load of fun while doing it.

THE GRIT TO SAY "FUCK YOU!"

I don't have to say "Fuck you" to anyone very often, but when I do say it, I am gladder than a dog chasing a ball that I have it in my bag of quick comebacks. I love it when I can say it with calm and determination. Think of all of the things you would be glad to say "Fuck you" to. Racism, stupidity, bullying, failing at something, a dick of a partner, a bad marriage, addiction, and especially when someone is being critical of you because of your age, gender, preferences, lifestyle, clothes, and so on.

Do you remember the recent incident in San Francisco where a seventy-six-year-old Asian woman was punched in the stomach by some racist asshole? She grabbed a board and whacked him with it. Well, that was a "Fuck you" whack for sure, even if she didn't say it. Yep, grab those boards and let 'em rip.

The good thing is that you do not even need to say it out loud. You can be in the presence of a rude, belligerent jerk and feel the need to stand there quietly, but inside you can be saying (with a smile, of course) "Fuck you, bastard." I have done this on airplanes and in traffic jams, grocery stores, restaurants, and even church.

Even if someone says it to you, remember to remain as calm as a lake on a lazy summer day. When their rant is finished, simply smile and thank them for sharing and walk away or turn away or get away the best you can without giving them any satisfaction.

The best firsthand example of this happened a few years ago, when I was walking down a sidewalk and happened to walk across the driveway to a grocery store. A woman drove up fast in her car, wanting to get out of the parking lot. I didn't stop but kept walking my brisk walk. The woman yelled out, "You stupid fucking asshole bitch!" and I replied, "Thank you for sharing," at which point she honked and honked and told me to "shut up." I hope she had a nice day.

Feel free to say it to yourself too, when you find yourself doing something out of line with your moral compass.

THE GRIT TO LAUGH AT YOURSELF!

Don't you love to laugh and even hear people laugh? If someone doesn't like your laugh or criticizes it for any reason, then pull out your "Fuck you" in any way you see fit. Think how much better life would be if all of those yellers and bellowers and puffed-up egos screaming at us were laughing instead. I could go for that.

Sometimes we find it easier to laugh at others than at ourselves, and that comes really close to bullying in my book. Nope. Don't do it. Learning to laugh at ourselves is like a glass of cold water on a hot Florida day. Refreshing, invigorating, and needed. Lighten up, for yourself and others. I also like to use laughter as a recovery mechanism when things have been falling into the "oh shit" category more than the "yippee" category. And humor is everywhere: kids, pets, books, TV, YouTube videos, and so on.

Betty White is one person who pokes my funny bone by just hearing her. In January 2021, she celebrated her ninety-ninth birthday. "Celebrate" is the important word here. And the world celebrated with her. She had an eighty-year career in radio and TV and still kept a great sense of humor. She wanted to be a forest ranger—wouldn't the National Parks have won on that one?—but she couldn't because she was a woman. Their loss and stupid mistake. Well, she did become an honorary ranger in 1988.

White said that she preferred looking at the bright side of life, as she didn't like the other side. She felt that being negative takes up too much energy and that you shouldn't take yourself too seriously. She said, "You can lie to others, not that I would, but you cannot lie to yourself." Good words of wisdom from someone who brought a lot of joy into the room.

Speaking of joy, in 2007 in England, a band called The Zimmers was formed. They had forty members between the ages of 71 and 102. They had talent too, and they shared it on the TV show *Britain's Got Talent*, made some records, and even came to the US in 2010 to perform for thirty-five hundred people.

They had lots of fun and brought happiness and laughter with them. So go out there and fall over laughing and bring some friends with you. It is great to laugh at the silly things we do and say all the time. Take that banana out of your butt and learn to laugh.

THE GRIT TO REINVENT
YOURSELF!

Does this mean you should be someone different from who you are? No, not at all. This means you should be your six-year-old self, your thirteen-year-old self, your twenty-nine-year-old self, your forty-two-year-old self, and all those in between. All of the good, the not-so-good, and the wish-it-didn't-happen. Because they all represent who you have become and will be.

Maybe your childhood was abusive, or your parents got divorced when you were a teenager, or your dad died in some faraway war. Maybe you flunked out of college or never had a chance to go. Maybe you acknowledged you are gay or trans-gender after being married and having children. Maybe your family business didn't do well and now you no longer speak to your relatives. I get it.

Do any of those things make you less you? They were all chal-lenges you ended up dealing with the best way you knew how at the time. You have this past, but you aren't your past. You are someone who tells the truth about who you are but doesn't use that past as an excuse.

The brilliant thing about reinventing yourself is that you start right now. This minute. And move forward. You look behind you and see a string of lights floating in the air, not a 747 attached to your shoulders that you are dragging along. Reinventing your-self doesn't have to be dramatic. It does need your purpose, consistency, and commitment.

Skilled Reinventors

Maybe you or someone you know has already reinvented them-self, so you know all about it. I can think of a few too. John Glenn was an astronaut for many years and then took what he knew about working with teams and setting goals and became a United States Senator for twenty-four years...and also went back into space.

Grandma Moses? She took up painting in her seventies because she could no longer do her favorite hobby, embroidery, due to her severe arthritis. She switched her creative endeavors from one love to something else she was good at doing.

Estella Pyfrom had so many achievements and accomplish-ments during her fifty-plus years of service for education and making life better for the people in her community that it would take pages to name them. She could have retired and been wonderfully proud of everything she had accomplished and everyone she had helped throughout her long career, but instead, she looked around and saw the need for something she could provide.

She wanted to create a project to help underprivileged families and children achieve a better quality of life through education and technology. Out of her commitment and expertise, she created Project Aspiration, better known as Estella's Brilliant Bus.

It really is a bus. Or, more accurately, it is a customized mobile learning center that travels around to communities in her Flor-ida area. The bus gives children and adults opportunities for self-paced education. And Estella sees more buses in the future as the success of this project gains momentum. Who knows what else this creative wonder can come up with to make lives better?

THE GRIT TO PUT YOURSELF FIRST!

This is difficult for many people, especially women. Yes, we were raised to be humble and not want things for ourselves, and we hear the echo of "don't be selfish" from our childhood. Hey, that was then, and this is now. Let that go. Learn how to say "no" and stick to it or say "hell yes" and go for it.

I cannot tell you how many single women and couples are literally raising their grandchildren and great-grandchildren even though the parents are perfectly able to do so themselves. These adult children have gotten used to and feel entitled to the free labor. The people taking advantage of you aren't always family. Others may have expectations of you due to church obligations, volunteer expectations, or cultural beliefs.

Recently, I have been reading articles about adult children who have moved back in with parents, do not have a job, and are verbally abusive and disrespectful. I have experience with that also. Sometimes you will end up taking drastic measures, like moving away or downsizing.

Example of Putting Yourself First

Ever heard of Ida Keeling? Ida Keeling's husband died at forty-two, and then her two sons were murdered within a couple of years of each other, which plummeted her into a deep depression. At sixty-seven, she started running after getting encouragement from her daughter to do some exercise.

She ran her first five-kilometer run and was thrilled with how she felt, so she kept on going. She set records for her age group in the sixty- and one-hundred-meter races. Then, thinking she might be too old, when she was ninety-nine, she told her doctor that she might not run anymore. He asked her why she would do that because there wasn't anything wrong with her.

He also suggested she have a shot of Hennessy each day for circulation. She took his advice and sometimes even put it in her morning coffee. Now, that's my kind of gal. When asked what her secret to a long life was, Ida—who lived to be 106—said, "The key to living long is to love yourself." And to do that, you need to put yourself first so you have what you need to love and take care of yourself.

THE GRIT TO KEEP GOING!

This is where you can show what you are made of when the shit hits the fan. If you have lived this long, you know bad times do cycle through life. You have probably had instances where you had to be your best even when you were at your worst.

Most people who have had children or people they love have had to do this. It didn't matter if you were tired, sick, exhausted, embarrassed, conflicted, hungry, dirty, or unprepared; you did it. Sometimes others knew, and many times they did not. Most of the time, you did it for other people, and sometimes that was what kept you going.

Remarkable Perseverance Examples

Priscilla Sitienei was a midwife in rural Kenya for sixty-five years before she chose to go to school when she was ninety years old to get an education. She wasn't able to go to school when she was growing up and had always wanted to learn to read and write. She also wanted to be able to write down her experiences and knowledge to pass down to others.

She put on her uniform and went to classes with six of her great-great-grandchildren. She certainly showed she had the grit to keep going. Age was just a number to her, and it didn't stop her from achieving a lifelong goal.

Harry Bernstein was an author and amazing man. I think I'm writing this book when I'm old, but Harry wrote his autobiographical and first book, *The Invisible*, when he was ninety-seven. This book was about the difficult childhood he had growing up in a poor Jewish neighborhood with an abusive father. Then he wrote about his family coming to America in *The Dream* when he was ninety-eight. He wrote his final book, *The Golden Willow*, when he was ninety-nine. This story was a tribute to his wife, Ruby, and his lifetime of love for her.

Talking about that book and his life in general, he said, "If I had not lived until I was ninety, I would not have been able to write this book... It could not have been done, even when I was ten years younger. I wasn't ready. God knows what other potentials lurk in other people, if we could only keep them alive well into their nineties." That was grit that you had, Harry. I would like to tell him that if all goes well and people realize their potential and find their purpose, there will be millions of people who will be able to share their wisdom and experiences in their nineties and beyond.

Let's talk about the radical grit example of Ruth Bader Ginsburg. She is an example of the grit to keep going for sure. President Clinton appointed her to serve on the Supreme Court in 1993. From that time until the beginning of the 2018 term, she did not miss a day of oral arguments. Not when she was having chemotherapy for pancreatic cancer, or after surgery for colon cancer, or even the day after her husband died in 2010. She was there working for us to make our lives better as she said she would do.

I know millions of people have had to flee for their lives from oppression, wars, slavery, and death, and they had the grit to keep going too. But that is a different kind of grit than we are talking about here, and I hope none of us have to endure anything like that as we experience the second half of our lives.

THE GRIT TO BE A WARRIOR!

This one is for you: the warrior you are and will continue to be. I've listed some things I feel make a warrior, and as you grow and live your purpose, you will add to this list. Obviously, I don't mean a literal warrior, although they certainly have many of the traits we want. Native Americans have warriors and elders, and they also have much advice and wisdom to give us. So do the wise people of other cultures.

A warrior **accepts the call** and takes the long, sometimes difficult, path of reaching their full potential.

A warrior **questions authority** and **makes up their own mind** based on what they know to be true from the knowledge of scientists and experts in their field.

A warrior **respects** all worldviews, all religions, all cultures, all histories, and all legacies, whether or not they believe in them or agree with them.

A warrior **believes that listening** is more important than speaking.

A warrior **is compassionate** and able to place themself in another's shoes for better understanding.

A warrior knows that contribution for good leaves generations to come with strong foundations.

A warrior **is strong** mentally, physically, and spiritually.

A warrior is someone who **does no harm**.

A warrior knows when to let the silence speak.

A warrior aligns to virtues, values, and purpose, not to human beings.

A warrior **lives the path of mastery**, which is always unfolding.

A warrior **speaks their truth** with compassion.

A warrior expands the tenderness of their heart.

A warrior **honors** the self and others.

A warrior's work is never done.

As I was writing out what it means to me to be a warrior, I had to step back for a moment and ask myself if I could truly say I was a warrior. For the most part, I can answer yes.

Not all of the time or in all circumstances, but these traits are things I think about every day, especially when my integrity or what I think is right gets challenged.

THOUGHT EXERCISE / ACTION STEP

Make a list of things that you feel make you gritty. Add to your list as you grow and live your purpose.

Every day, I try to do no harm either verbally, physically, or even mentally to myself. Yes, it is often a huge challenge for me to keep my word. Your challenge now is to keep finding ways that you are gritty and share that self with the world, because it matters and you matter. This new kick-ass you is a world-changer. Thanks, grit! Now that you're equipped with the grit to make it through life's toughest moments, let's focus on wrapping this up so you can get started on the next step of your kick-ass journey!

YOUR KICK-ASS MANTRA

"My grit and commitment to myself is unbreakable."

Chapter 10

THE END IS YOUR BEGINNING

After all is said and done, and you have finished the book, it is time to take a deep breath and not think about it for a while. Okay, maybe just a few days. If you wait too long, you will never take the steps to get where you can be, which is in the kick-ass second half of your life. This is sort of like starting with a big slab of marble from which you have chipped away at all of the things that stood in the way of you creating a new vision for these next fifty years or so, and what you have is a polished, smooth, and remarkable work of genius.

It has been great sharing all of this with you, and I hope you have found value and inspiration. We really hammered through a lot of ways to get to where you want to be, starting from just looking at where you are now and what brought you to this place in your life. Stopping to think about that and evaluating the good and the not-so-good is a starting point.

Getting your life in order and looking at all the categories of your life can seem exhausting, but it also can give you great satisfaction, knowing what you have planned is truly something that you created. It is your vision and not what someone else wants you to be or do. I really want to stress the importance of taking your time to work through some of these areas, as clarity will come as you put the pieces together. Because you have worked on getting time to work for you rather than marching to its tick-tock, you will have all the time you need to follow through on your vision and pursue your purpose.

As I mentioned before, depending on where you are on this journey, you might need a few gap years to wander, physically and mentally. Recovery and rejuvenation are both part of reaching our peak performance. And if you don't recover and rejuvenate, I can guarantee stress and anxiety will come and bite you on the butt or some other uncomfortable place. Remember, you might need to put on the blinders and learn to say no when it is time to focus. Just do it with compassion and honesty, and people will be very supportive. If they aren't, then you know what you have to do.

When you think about creativity and what you want to do with yours, please open the tap full out like a fire hose. Let it rip and bounce you around like a child and drench you with all the stuff you have been holding inside, afraid to let it out. I get a newsletter from Phil Town, author and financial wizard, and he always ends with "Go Play." I love that. And that's what I want you to do too. Consider playing a lot. With your thoughts and your attitude and your creativity. Try new things all the time. Be a little bit crazy or a lot.

Do a check on your attitudes, your state of mind, what words you speak, and how you communicate with people. Are you compassionate or a little bit put out and angry? Do you find yourself being judgmental and critical or minding your own business and being present with whatever is going on? Don't label your thoughts good or bad; just be aware of it and decide if it's working for you and how you want to be in the world. And if you find yourself trying to take huge bites out of your Dagwood sandwich of motivation and you just cannot cram it all in at once, then eat it like you would an elephant. One bite at a time. Even a bite is a lot to digest, and that's why all those lists were in the book. Hang on to your lists too and look at them periodically, as you will want to make changes.

Take that grit test every few months and see how you do, or make up your own categories. The test was originally for students, so the results will be different for you. But grit is something you can develop even if you are an introvert and not very good with people. The world needs introverts. And don't forget to use your lifetime supply of "Fuck you" whenever life calls for it. I want you to have fun becoming a warrior and noting all the things that put you in that category. Make it yours and be proud. Every time you conquer some fear, stand up to a bully, take a stand, or call out an injustice, note it on your warrior shield. As you gather strength, it will make you even more aware and able to deal with whatever comes your way.

I see a future of thousands of warriors living a brilliant second half of life, using their purpose and passion to make the world a better place and to leave a road map and manual for future generations to continue to work together, solve problems that make people's lives better, and heal the Earth by being stewards rather than destroyers.

Now that our lives are working the way we want them, or we have a plan that moves us in that direction, it is time to look at how we will work with groups of people who have the same passions and convictions we have rather than being forced to work with groups that feel they have to work together.

"Want to" versus "have to" is the important difference here. There are hundreds of opportunities to join up with groups of people doing good work within the community of people over fifty or sixty. I will be sharing with you my experiences and recommendation in the Resources section, but just know this is only a sample. Finding what is right for you might require experimenting and trying out a few new opportunities before something clicks.

Keep your purpose and passion in mind and lean into those situations that speak to you and help you meet other people who share your interests.

I've been focused mostly on getting this book finished, but I have also been looking at places for possible trainings for two to three weeks. I realized that if people are coming from all over the world, I need to be within an hour of an international airport, so that has narrowed my search.

I've also been talking with facilitators to help with groups, I am in contact with several international organizations with a multinational staff, and I am finding out how all of this works.

I don't know about you, but my work with groups hasn't always been successful, to put it mildly. However, it will be especially important to figure out what does work when our groups consist of talented people from around the world with different cultures and ways of doing things. The good news is that much work has been done documenting what does work.

I am particularly interested in the research of R. Keith Sawyer, author of *Group Genius: The Creative Power of Collaboration* and *Zig Zag: The Surprising Path to Greater Creativity*. In *Group Genius*, Sawyer discusses ten conditions for group flow that I feel are an excellent starting point for the work that needs to be done. The conditions include things like how to make sure everyone understands the goal and how to listen for clarity. He also discusses the blending of egos and making sure everyone participates equally while emphasizing easy and free-flowing communication and familiarity with each other.

Sawyer did a lot of research with sports teams, jazz ensembles, and improvisational theater groups, but his findings would also work well with groups made up of diverse people from many cultures. You can see how necessary it will be for the project groups to spend time together getting to know one another, finding a common communication style, and understanding what needs to be done.

Facilitators will be specially trained in handling these dynamic groups and making sure everyone is heard and understood and appreciated for their contributions. And if you are part of a group, you will bring your own set of skills and experiences to enhance the process.

I see us as creators, planners, inventors, problem solvers, and directors, not necessarily the doers. Most of the initial work, the planning, and the creative process can be done via online meetings after the groups are formed. However, I also see onsite work that might last for weeks or even months, and we will deal with all of that as things unfold.

This is why I need your creative genius too. It is going to take many of us to make this happen. And I definitely don't know what I don't know.

I'm also gathering data on various projects around the world and what types of help they need, as well as their timelines. And of course, funding will need to be acquired for all aspects of the work we will be doing.

We're going to need everyone, from chefs to bricklayers, engineers to electricians, knitters to gardeners, and plumbers to doctors. Yes, and everything in-between. Teams have to be put together and trained, and that also takes a special talent. So let's see what you've got.

I see this next phase as challenging, unpredictable, rewarding, and experimental. This is where we will learn what we don't know and be creative in how we find out. And I need you there with me on the journey.

To get started in this new community, make sure I have your email address and other information so I can keep you updated with newsletters. I will be sending out a questionnaire asking you about your skills and interests and where you think work needs to be done.

I will want to inform you of where you are needed, what projects are available, and the best way for you to get involved. I also want to hear what you are doing and how your journey is unfolding for you in the second half of life.

I'm on Facebook and Instagram. And I even have that Twitter thing and LinkedIn. My email is Kathleen@KathleenSinclair.com, and I have a website that you can connect with me through as well: www.KathleenSinclair.com.

I encourage you to leave a review on Amazon if you purchased this book through them. They love to chomp the bits, spit out information, and hand out treats.

Go get 'em!

YOUR KICK-ASS MANTRA

"My mind is brilliant. My body is healthy. My spirit is tranquil. I'm fully committed to living a kick-ass life every single day."

RESOURCES

This chapter is full of my own examples and experiences, but also suggestions to get you started in the right direction. In other words, this chapter is full of resources I wish I had known about when I started my journey in my fifties. I hope this helps you along your path to your kick-ass life!

LONG-TERM VOLUNTEER EXPERIENCE

When I was sixty-three, I went into the Peace Corps. It is a twenty-seven-month commitment where you train for three months and learn a new language, live with a host family, do work similar to what you will be doing on your own, and then go to your site for two years.

I went to Ukraine, near the Russian border—the part that was lost to Russia a few years ago. They still spoke Russian even though the Soviet Union had fallen apart in 1991. I had traveled a lot and lived in other countries for a short time, but I had never worked in another country, and that was something I wanted to do to dive deeper into a culture and history and learn about the people in a way I could not do as a tourist, no matter how long I stayed there.

The Peace Corps provided that working experience through a structure that was already set up and had been running for a long time. That was a plus for me. It provided a safety net for those areas I needed, like training, healthcare, and a support system. I was in Ukraine from 2008 to 2010, so things could be a lot different now, and you could talk with a thousand Peace Corps volunteers who served in the same country, and you would hear a thousand different stories.

I taught at a pedagogical university in a city of about 120,000 people and lived in the dormitory with the students. I was the only native-English-speaking person teaching there, and the staff relied on me to speak to many people and groups. They were still using Soviet textbooks and materials, but through grants that I wrote, I was able to get them a computer lab and updated materials and equipment.

The students were amazing, but many of the teachers thought I was a spy and didn't trust me. They weren't familiar with volunteerism and could not understand why an older woman would leave her life in the US and go there to teach unless there was something else going on.

As you can imagine, I learned a lot more than the students did, and it was a rewarding and valuable experience that changed the way I thought about myself and other people. So if you are inclined toward serving your country, learning about another culture, providing experience and skills to a group of people who will benefit, and can leave the US for over two years, then I highly recommend it.

MEDIATION AND CONFLICT RESOLUTION

The Peace Corps experience led me into another opportunity I explored and still use today: mediation and conflict resolution. I find I am using this more and more as I end up in conversations about politics, Black Lives Matter, climate change, and other issues that are pulling us apart.

While working in a post-USSR republic, I found that there was a huge Soviet influence on all of the generations that lived under that regime. My students were the first generation to live with democracy, but many older people longed for the days of Soviet rule where they got vouchers for their sofas, cars, apartments, and food.

They felt they were educated and middle class, and then one day, they woke up and the Soviet Union was no more. Now they lived in a poor country and no longer had the perks they had become accustomed to, and their middle-class status had dissolved before them. I knew nothing of their lives except what they shared with me, but I knew listening was where I could excel. And listening is a big part of conflict resolution and mediation.

If you are interested at all in learning more about the legal system, learning how to run a good meeting, bringing people together, seeing a situation from all sides, or helping people navigate the legal system to deal with a problem, then this might be something you could get into.

My path to mediation and conflict resolution was via university classes that led to a certificate. However, that is no longer necessary, as many court systems offer these classes, as do private industries. It took me about a year to get the certificate. Following this, I did an internship for six months and then I worked right in the system. I participated in small claims disputes, juvenile crime cases, neighborhood disagreements, and some family issues. I found it extremely rewarding and beneficial, and it really helps the courts to have trained, experienced volunteers they can count on.

HOME AND PET SITTING

If you want to travel and want some kind of home stay, but don't want to work in another country, then I recommend house and pet sitting. I traveled the world and did this for a year. I specifically looked for longer sits, as I didn't want to be moving around a lot and I wanted to get to know an area. The shortest gig I had was for three weeks and the longest was three months. Most of the others were a month.

I didn't get to know the people because I came, we exchanged information about what they wanted me to do, and then it was just me and the pets. It was heaven for me, as I love dogs and cats. I also took care of chickens, rabbits, a horse, some goats, and a few birds.

There is a ton of information about this online, and really, the sites make it easy. You will want to plan out your route or how to weave sits together, or where you might like to go in between assignments. Experienced sitters have done it all and are most helpful in answering questions and concerns.

There usually isn't any money exchanged, and you need to pay your own way to get to the destination.

OTHER OPTIONS

There is a lot of good work going on around the world, and there are many opportunities for helping out through teaching, healthcare, agriculture, technology, and basically any area you can think of. I haven't worked with Habitat for Humanity, but they have local as well as international opportunities, and you can apply as an individual.

I will admit here that in comparison with many older people, I seem to have an advantage because I am not fearful, and I am willing to live with not always knowing what is going to happen next and a level of discomfort. Plus that curiosity gene keeps me interested, and I am good at improvising.

I wasn't always like that, and doing what I talk about in this book has given me more confidence as well as skills and intuition about people, places, and situations. And following some of my suggestions will get you there too.

Maybe jumping into something by yourself seems too scary or uncomfortable for you. Those are real concerns. Talk with other people who are out doing things and see what they have experienced and what the ups and downs are from their point of view.

You might have to go outside your group of friends to find people who have done things you are interested in doing. Sometimes that is a good idea anyway. I love my friends, but there are very few of them I would want to travel with or explore new areas of interest with.

VOLUNTEERING

Volunteering can be to your advantage, especially when your interests are different from those of others. Friends can be well-meaning, but if what you want to do isn't something they would do, then chances are they aren't going to give you the kind of feedback you need in order to make decisions. The more you are out there being curious and asking questions, the more people you will meet and the more opportunities you will have to test out whether you want to do a particular thing or not. Volunteering can give you a window into what really goes on in an organization.

But "What the hell?" you say. You don't particularly like to travel or are tired of having to do it for your job, or you just want to find out more about the area you just moved to. Lately, when I talk with people about what I am doing, they tell me they admire my energy but they are homebodies.

They might be homebodies, but they are some of the smartest people I know, and spending time with them always leaves me with new ideas and possibilities. Being a homebody is good. And if that is what works for you, then do it with all of your heart.

THE IMPACT OF COVID

The COVID pandemic knocked the air out of me. At first, I felt like a victim of an unseeable enemy. Fear, anxiety, grouchiness, and an unsettled feeling followed me around and clung to me like Velcro. But gradually, I realized it was an opportunity and I shouldn't pass it up for the inconvenience it might cause me. And really, it wasn't much of an inconvenience. Sure, I had to wear a mask when I went for food, groceries, gas, and other staples, but so what?

I was busy doing research and writing this book, and as nasty as that invisible enemy was, the pandemic gave me more time to do what I wanted to be doing. I took the time to look into organizations made up of elders and working with elders to create change and address the issues facing humanity at this time.

When starting out on your journey to peak performance and living your passion and purpose, it is often helpful to be a part of a group that is already doing some of the same things you are interested in doing rather than trying to go it alone.

The nice thing about where we are now is that most of the meetings are via Zoom or a webinar, so you have time to listen and maybe ask questions in the chat feature and look at the people and see if you connect with them, all from the safety of your own home. And you can click off anytime you want. No questions.

OPPORTUNITIES AND RESOURCES FOR
THE SECOND HALF OF LIFE GROUP

If you are who I think you are, then you already know of many groups, networks, organizations, or committees you enjoy being part of. However, I remember a friend saying that "you speak to the choir but leave the windows open." And that is what I am doing here for those of you who haven't had the opportunity yet to get out and share your amazing self.

The next few examples are groups that cater to people just like us. Read through these and see what clicks. You can always go to their websites and find out more or google them and see what pops up. As you know, I am not an active social media partici-pant, but I have really learned a lot about organizations by look-ing at their social media and reading the comments.

It often feels like technology is a one-way conversation, and it is a lot different from speaking to others in person. And then there is the delay in responses. But the more you use these different platforms and new ways of "getting together," the more familiar they become.

Pour the wine, invite the kids to teach you, and dig into some of this technology stuff so you feel comfortable looking into the next group. Have fun here.

Elders Action Network

Elders Action Network (EAN) says on their website, "We're building a movement of elders to address the social and environmental crises of our time!" Well, hello. Sign me up. I just listened to a town-hall meeting for sound democracy, and one of the narrators said they were looking for "people who have come alive." That is what I call a direct call to action.

EAN has community conversations that focus on social justice issues and climate chaos. They also have online workshops and book study groups. You can participate with groups promoting sound democracy, climate action, regenerative living, and social justice. EAN has a newsletter, a journal, national events, plus a whole lot more.

Encore Nonprofit

Another group I found out about in my research is the Encore nonprofit. Their website says, "Encore.org was founded on the belief that the aging of America isn't so much a problem to be solved as it is an opportunity to be seized." They have worked for over twenty years to create a movement around second acts for years fifty and beyond—an encore in the lives of older, inspired, enthusiastic, and brilliant people.

They have had many reasons to be proud of their work over the years since their founder, Marc Freedman, coined the term "encore career." Marc Freedman wrote *How to Live Forever: The Enduring Power of Connecting the Generations,* and Marci Alboher, author and vice president at Encore.org, wrote *The Encore Career Handbook: How to Make a Living and a Difference in the Second Half of Life.* I highly recommend both books.

Encore has a program where adults tutor in underserved public schools, and their results are worth looking into. They have also invested millions in social innovators over sixty who are creating a better future for everyone.

What I find remarkable is their program on *paid* midlife internships with nonprofit organizations to help people transition to a career in the social sector. So far, according to their website, "2,000+ fellows have provided more than 2 million hours of service, at a fraction of their market value, contributing the equivalent of more than $200 million to not-for-profit organizations in over 50 metropolitan areas." They really do live their vision. Particularly pay attention to the *paid* internships.

American Association of Retired Persons (AARP)

Of course you have heard of AARP, as they magically seem to know just when you turn fifty and start sending you magazines. But they are a whole lot more than their magazine. They have more than sixty thousand volunteers who donate their time and talent, and you could be one of them. They have programs, like Experience Corps (where you teach others what you know), Legal Counsel, and Elder Watch, to name a few. Under their Causes, they have healthcare and wellness, fraud prevention, diversity and inclusion, veterans and military families, and the list goes on.

These groups really embrace the pleasures and excitement of growing older and certainly shift away from the negative stuff you might hear about aging. They speak right to a lot of the concerns you might have about checking out new things and getting involved.

Wait, I thought I heard someone say, "Hold on, Kathleen, my mind is filled up and I can't take on anymore. I just want to drink wine, check on my geraniums, and maybe eat that carton of Ben and Jerry's chocolate raspberry swirl!" Okay, I agree that this is a bit much to take in all at once.

I'm cramming it all in here so you have a resource. That doesn't mean you have to absorb everything at once. Just chew off bits now and leave the rest for another time. I'm on a mission here to give you as much information and possibility as I can, and I don't want to cut short some amazing opportunities.

So, you do what you need to do, and I will do what I need to do. Okay? And when we meet, I will buy the drinks.

Next Avenue

Next Avenue provides an opportunity to get inspiration and continue your education through listening and reading.

Next Avenue has a mission "to meet the needs and unleash the potential of older Americans through the power of media." Their articles, written by journalists and experts, cover every aspect of growing older and doing it well. They are part of PBS, so you know they are delivering quality material.

I find their newsletters very beneficial and am always forwarding them to friends. They welcome hearing from people and want to know what you are thinking about. They also hand out yearly awards to people who are making a difference in the lives of older people.

TED Talks and Podcasts

Don't forget about TED Talks and podcasts for inspiration and great advice. There are many geared specifically to the issues and questions of people over fifty. If you are lucky enough to live near a university, find out about all of the activities and programs they have for adults. These are usually outstanding and well worth your time.

Senior Scholars

I used to live in Charlotte, North Carolina, and Queens University has a wonderful program called Senior Scholars for people over fifty. They often have over 350 people in attendance. The speakers stay after their talk and answer questions. Plus, it is a great place to meet and see people weekly and dive into lively discussions. See if something like that is available in your area.

SCORE, Executive Service Corps, and CIRKEL

There are also opportunities to use your skills in various fields to mentor others, and I want to remind you that using retired executives and business owners to help new leaders and entrepreneurs isn't new. SCORE (Service Corps of Retired Executives) has been bringing their knowledge and expertise in the form of mentorship since 1964. The Executive Service Corps, started in Chicago in 1978, provides free or low-cost consulting to over 150 nonprofit organizations.

CIRKEL is a newer organization, started in 2018. On their website, they state that they are "a platform connecting a community of professionals ages 20–70+ who connect for a two-way career support and mentorship. CIRKEL also works with businesses to unite the 5-generation workforce." That is the first time I have heard of uniting the five generations working together, and I really like the concept.

TEACHING AND LEARNING

I know that some of you have amazing skills and teaching abilities and might want to hook up with one of the organizations I have mentioned if they are in your area. Don't forget about teaching at a community college or a community education program through your local parks and recreation department. These are also things you can do with friends and have a lot of fun. Think cake baking, Italian cooking, small engine repair, gardening, hair cutting, dog grooming, pickle making, or figuring out Excel so you don't want to shoot yourself. You get the idea. Anything goes.

MAKING MONEY

Okay, you have probably realized that with so many people launching into the second half of life, there have to be some badass opportunities for making the big bucks. And you are absolutely correctamundo. But we have to get ourselves organized and prepared, and that doesn't mean taking it easy. It is this next group that really speaks to me and where I see us making our biggest inroads. So let's have a look.

According to Stanford researchers, 31 percent of people aged fifty to ninety-two "identify, prioritize, adopt and actively pursue goals that are both personally meaningful and contribute to the greater good." And that, dear friends, is 34 million people and counting. Now, I find volunteering an exciting way to meet people, do valuable work, and find out just what interests you. And it is a great way to spend time if you aren't quite sure of your purpose and passion but still want to do some good work and do it with wonderful, caring people.

However, if you are still looking for ways to contribute and want to explore how to make money, there are amazing things going on that you could tap into and investigate.

XPRIZE

According to Google, XPRIZE is a **nonprofit organization that designs and hosts public competitions** intended to encourage technological development to benefit humanity.

XPRIZE was the brainchild of Peter Diamandis, whose quote "The day before something is truly a breakthrough, it's a crazy idea," sums it up. You can get involved as an individual, a group, a company, a startup, or an innovator.

They are passionate about creating "a world where everyone's days are spent imagining, creating, and collaborating, not fearing and fighting. A world where everyone has access to clean water, nutritious food, affordable housing, effective learning, top-tier medical care, and non-polluting, abundant energy." Here are some of the prizes.

Feed the Next Billion: a four-year, $15 million prize

Carbon Removal: fighting climate change with $100 million, funded by Elon Musk

Rainforest: a five-year, $10 million prize to understand the rainforest ecosystem

Rapid Reskilling: a thirty-month, $5 million prize to reskill under-resourced workers

Pretty amazing, don't you think? Can you see yourself and a team of experts just like you working on these kinds of projects? It gives me goosebumps. There is tons of information on their website, on Google, and in lots of other places too. Read up.

The Audacious Project

Another group dedicated to inspiring change is the Audacious Project, launched by TED. Every year they "nurture a group of big, bold solutions to the world's most urgent challenges and with the support of an inspiring group of donors and supporters come together to get them launched." Here are some projects they have funded.

What if we built a global surveillance network to stop the next pandemic before it starts?

What if we could lift millions of the world's poorest people out of ultra-poverty?

What if African farmers could end global extreme poverty in our lifetime?

What if life-saving prescriptions could be affordable for all Americans?

Holy crap, people. This is real stuff. We can do this kind of work too. This is such an opportunity for who we will be during this next half of our kick-ass lives.

Bezos Earth Fund and the Solutions Project

The Bezos Earth Fund has given $791 million to climate groups, NGOs, and conservation groups, and one of them I had never heard of. The Solutions Project invests in a "climate justice movement that centers women and power-building organizations led by Black, Indigenous, Immigrant, and other people of color" to have access to 100 percent clean energy and equitable access to healthy air, water, and land.

Their feeling is that the people closest to the problems often have the solutions, but they don't have the money or a way to tell people what they know. And even though pollution and climate change affect people of color and women to a greater degree, only 0.6 percent of all foundation donations goes toward women of color. If this kind of work speaks to your heart, the Solutions Project could use your support.

Do some research, and the next time you are with a group of friends or even people you don't know very well, see what happens if you bring up these challenges. Pay attention to who asks questions, who is skeptical, who tries to change the subject, and who asks for more information. Right there you will get a few people who feel the same excitement you do. They are your potential team.

MODERN ELDER ACADEMY (MEA)

If you need time and a place to nurture your ideas and get support mentally, spiritually, and physically, and you have the resources, think about going to one of the retreats offered by Modern Elder Academy. "MEA provides an environment for people to reimagine midlife as a time for learning, growth, and positive transformation through immersive workshops and sabbaticals."

Their campus is currently in Baja, Mexico, and they have announced they will be opening a campus near Santa Fe, New Mexico, in the near future. The typical age is forty-five to sixty-five, but their participants range in age from thirty to eighty-eight. The founder, Chip Conley, said, "I wanted to create a place where people could get the tools and support to feel confident and inspired in the second half of their adult life." What a great place to go by yourself or with a group of people you want to bond with for future projects.

Please let me know of other organizations and opportunities so I can update my resources and share them with you. I know there are many more out there waiting to be discovered. This is just a small example of the creative and meaningful things happening right now, and together we can continue adding to the stories of inspiration and change.

APPENDIX

These are the thought exercises / action steps mentioned throughout the book.

CHAPTER 1

Make a list of all of the words you have been called, heard other people called, or heaven forbid, you have called people you think are "old." Include words that you have called yourself in this list. You know, those times when you put yourself down, whether it was out loud or as that lovely inner voice that constantly shows up.

* * *

Here's an interesting little side exercise for you: take a moment to pause and write down how long will you live. And by live, I mean be healthy, have a sound mind, and be able to contribute to society. Take that number and put it away somewhere with the date on it. You can and will look at it later on.

CHAPTER 2

Examine whether or not you keep your word to yourself. Inevitably, there are times when you don't. Make three columns on a sheet of paper. In the first, write the situations where you don't keep your word. In the second, write down why you don't. In the third, write down what you will do to keep your word based on each newfound realization.

Be honest. Come on, no one is going to see this but you. You might find that some of the things you promise yourself really aren't that important and you can remove them from your self-promise list.

* * *

Make four columns on a sheet of paper. In column one, mark down every time you complain about something for one week. In column two, list the date and time of those complaints. In column three, write what you complained about, and in column four, list your reason for complaining. No judgment here. Write down anything at all that falls into the category of complaining.

To get into the habit, you can start without the specifics by simply keeping a tally. Write it on the back of your hand, and at the end of each day, your eyes will be opened up when your entire arm is marked up with complaint tallying. It is way more powerful if you write down what you actually complain about, but right now, I just want you to become aware of how often you are doing this.

* * *

Keep a gratitude journal. The best way to dive in is to start by thinking of one thing. What is one tiny little thing to be grateful for? Even if you think your life is a huge pile of the steaming brown icky stuff...what about breathing as an example of something for which you can be grateful? Try writing down one thing you are grateful for each day for one week. Then make a 100 percent jump and try writing down two things you are grateful for during the second week. And so on. You've got this. Do it.

* * *

Write out the top five worst fears you have related to assumptions. For example, "My worst fear is that someone will figure out I am a fraud or assume I don't know what I am doing at this new job." After you write out five, write out a kick-ass turnaround for each: "I'm very talented and deserve this job!" Using this kind of kick-ass turnaround thinking will help you cancel out the assumption before it takes over. If you happen to remember any assumptions from your past, write those down too. Maybe you made an assumption about this book or you made an assumption about your partner. Whatever you remember, write it down. The more you explore, the higher you'll soar.

* * *

Make a list of every single thing that you haven't fully dealt with in your home or office that keeps taking up brain space. These irritations and naggings won't go away unless you do something.

Write three columns on your sheet of paper. At the top of one, write, "Things that irritate me so much I want to kick something." At the top of the second one, write, "Delegate to." And at the top of the third one, write, "By when."

So, it might go like this: The screen door is broken. The screen is ripped, has holes, and flaps in the wind. Plus, mosquitoes and bugs are always getting into the house. Do you have the skills to fix it? Do you even want to fix it? Do you think after twenty years that maybe a new one is in order? Would you be willing to pay someone to fix it? Who might that be? Could you find someone on Thumbtack or another online service? Do you have a bunch of things that need fixing like the screen? Maybe you can brainstorm for five minutes to fix a problem that irritates you every time you go out that door. Write down some ideas in the second column. Then, in the third column, write down a date. And not next year. Make it soon. The next couple of weeks would be great, no more than thirty days.

* * *

Think about things people have said to you in the past. If someone says something that niggles a tiny bit, like a mosquito buzzing your ear at 3:00 a.m., then for sweet baby Jesus's sake, do something about it. Look at it. Is what they said true? Is what they've brought up something that you love about yourself, or do you know it could use some tweaking? Does this fall into cleaning up some stuff? If yes, then do it. If not, then ignore it. Their business. Thank you very much.

* * *

Think about things you do in your life. Ask yourself, "Is there a better way to do this? Is there a tiny bit more I could do each time to make it easier for myself or for someone else?" Ask yourself questions; get curious with yourself. Getting curious with yourself means that you are always, always doing your best. If we train ourselves to do our best with things that aren't important to us, like everyday tasks, we will be setting ourselves up for doing our best all the time. That in itself will become a habit.

* * *

Whenever you are with a person who has to be right, but who you know is dead wrong, ask yourself a few questions:

1. Will anyone be hurt by this opinion?

2. Does it make any difference in the scheme of life?

3. Do I really give a damn if this person thinks they are right?

4. Am I willing to let it go, knowing that the truth of the matter is what counts?

Then hum a few lines of "Let It Go" and stop talking.

CHAPTER 3

Recall the four "mapping your vision" questions.

1. Start with what's true about yourself right now. Find out what your beliefs and assumptions are for each category. What is the concept and mental image you have of yourself in each area? Write out where you are currently at.

2. Next, write out how you see yourself in your ideal way.

3. Write out the reasons behind what you want to do in each category.

4. Finally, how the hell are you going to get there?

Use those four questions to define and map your vision in each of these main categories:

- Health and fitness, including food and drink

- Family

- Parenting

- Love life

- Intellectual interests

- Spiritual and religious interests

Add your own categories if you feel any additional categories are needed.

CHAPTER 4

Recall the four "mapping your vision" questions.

1. Start with what's true about yourself right now. Find out what your beliefs and assumptions are for each category. What is the concept and mental image you have of yourself in each area? Write out where you are currently at.

2. Next, write out how you see yourself in your ideal way.

3. Write out the reasons behind what you want to do in each category.

4. Finally, how the hell are you going to get there?

Use those four questions to define and map your vision in each of these main categories:

- Social

- Financial

- Career

- Quality of life

- Relationships outside of family

- Contribution to society

Also add or subtract any categories that don't apply to you or that you find unnecessary.

CHAPTER 5

Figure out what kind of a person you are: productive or just busy. Decide whether or not you want to do anything about it. If you feel that things are going great, then carry on. If you don't like what happens to your time, then you have some choices to make.

* * *

Figure out a reasonable amount of time to do something and get it done in that amount of time.

* * *

Identify your time vampires. Develop an action plan for dealing with them. Delegate if necessary.

* * *

1. Examine your routines (e.g., morning, evening). What can you do to save yourself time? Write these things down and then do them.

2. Make a list of things to never do again.

3. Make a list of what you want to do with your 86,400 seconds of time each day.

CHAPTER 6

No actions steps here. I suggest taking a break and having a nice cup of tea.

CHAPTER 7

Wow, none of those action steps here either. Don't worry, you make up for it in the next chapter. Better get something stronger to drink.

CHAPTER 8

Grab a pen and paper. Yes, yet again. It is one of the most effective ways to get things done and to help you remember. You can use sticky notes or index cards. Write down ten to twenty-five things you are curious about. You will need to broaden your curiosity scope beyond things like "I'm curious about the weather this weekend" or "I wonder what to serve those twenty people coming for dinner on Saturday."

Curious in this sense means if you had a weekend or two to read a couple of books, watch a program, or talk with someone who is an expert in a particular field, who, where, and what would this be? More than just a passing inquiry, this is something that grabs your attention. It is motivational energy.

You are looking for new and challenging topics, topics that you want to and can become fully absorbed in, to the point where you are willing to devote time and thought to answer some of your questions. You will need this kind of energy to push away distractions that want to buzz in your ear like that nighttime mosquito.

There will be eight more action steps in this chapter, so get ready.

* * *

You are going to want to visualize these twenty-five curiosities, and there are several ways you can do that. I have used sticky notes and index cards, but pieces of paper will do fine, or making two columns on a piece of paper with your curiosities on one side will work as well.

If you are using sticky notes, get yourself a big piece of paper or use your dining room table. Think big. Draw (or visualize) a circle large enough so that you can place these twenty-five sticky notes (or however many you end up with) around the circle at even intervals. Then number the sticky notes and their location on the paper. If this seems confusing, have a glass of wine and read on. If you are using index cards, just lay them out in rows so you can see everything at one time. The next thing you want to do is hunt for intersections.

* * *

Study all of your curiosities and see if they overlap or are in any way related to other things you have written down. If you drew a circle with sticky notes, draw a line from one to the other across the page, up and down, or however they combine. If you are using index cards, pretend you are playing solitaire and stack up those that are similar or are related in some way. You will end up with some that are related and a few that are just hanging out being interesting. Save those. But look at the ones that overlap—that is where you will find energy and possibility.

* * *

For the next step, after you have found your top curiosities and stacked them up into balls of energy, it is time to get to know these new ideas. This can take a month, a year, or in my case, multiple years.

Start by spending ten to fifteen minutes a day listening to a podcast or lecture, or watching a TED Talk or other video around your curiosity topics. You can also read articles and books. Feed your curiosities a little bit at a time, and watch as your brain brings things together and starts to see patterns and familiarities.

* * *

You will need to get out another piece of paper or continue working in your notebook.

Write down a list of ten to fifteen massive problems facing the world today that you would like to see solved. These should be things everyone has to deal with: climate change, hunger, homelessness, energy scarcity, environmental degradation. As you did with your curiosity list, try to be as specific as possible. This might require some research too. Most massive problems aren't just one problem, but thousands of smaller problems all lumped together. You will need to know what these are.

* * *

When you have this list, look for places where your passions intersect with these huge global problems. That intersection is a place where your passion is a solution to some huge problem. And if not the whole solution, then a portion of it. That is your purpose.

You could be looking at a great business opportunity, with or without partners, and a way to use your newfound passion to do some serious good in the world. This translates into your massive transformative purpose (MTP).

* * *

The big targets that we want to get to are called the high hard goals or the big goals. These goals are steps you will take to reach your MTP and may include getting a degree, starting a business, creating a nonprofit, or writing a book. High hard goals help us stay persistent, and they focus our attention. But damn, they are big. They will often feel uncomfortable, but that is how you know you have gone big. Go ahead and write some of these down. As you dive deeper, you will be adding to or subtracting from this list.

* * *

In come clear goals. Start writing these down for each of your high hard goals. Clear goals are all of the smaller steps we will take along the way to reach our high hard goals. These goals tell us when and where to put our attention. When our goals are as clear as a mountain lake, our mind doesn't have to wander around, trying to figure out what to do next. It already knows.

Non-important stuff gets filtered out, and action and awareness start to come together as our concentration gets more focused. Sounds good, doesn't it? Are you ready for the tricky part? The emphasis has to be on "clear" and not "goals." Clarity equals certainty, and that's what we want at this point. We need to know what to do and where to focus our attention.

Our day-to-day means breaking tasks down into bite-sized chunks and setting goals accordingly.

CHAPTER 9

Make a list of things that you feel make you gritty. Add to your list as you grow and live your purpose.

CHAPTER 10

Okay, last chance to do an action step, and this one is really important. Talk with you soon.

Contact me at kathleen@kathleensinclair.com or www. Kathleensinclair.com.

ACKNOWLEDGMENTS

I want to start by thanking my family, Karis, Jason, London, Sierra, Sharon, and Anissa, for hanging in there with me when I didn't answer the phone and wasn't available for a couple of years. Thanks for your patience.

A special thank you to my agent, publicist, and friend, Starr Hall Egan, for believing in me and pulling me out of a messy time in my life and knowing just what to do.

Gratitude and thanks to all of the wonderful individuals at Scribe Media who I worked with: publishing manager Erin Mellor; editor Nicole Jobe; cover designer Anna Dorfman; additional editors Holly Gorman and Cindi Angelini; and everyone else on the Scribe team who helped get this book out into the world.

Included with the wonderful Scribe people are the mentors on the weekly calls, Emily, Chas, and Hussein, as well as all of the writers sharing the good, the bad, and the ugly. I appreciate the insightful and personal advice.

I want a big happy shout-out to my writing buddies, Cath Knibbs, Heidi Weber, and Everett Goldner. Deepest gratitude for your honesty, humor, and confidence. I hope someday we can get together for a toast. And for Karen Darke, Michael Mannino, and the other facilitators and advisors at Flow for Writers. Included in this group is Clare Goodrich, who was with me from the beginning of my journey with the Flow Research Collective. Your encouragement meant a great deal to me.

To the advisors and mentors who have made a difference in my life and helped pave the way to getting this book published. They are, in no particular order, Steven Kotler and the team at the Flow Research Collective; Eric Edmeades and the Speaking Academy staff, who cajoled and worked with me so I could become a speaker; Jack Canfield and his team; Phil Town and his group of really smart cookies; JB Owen, who is a wonder in pink; Vishen Lakhiani and the mentors at Mindvalley; Dr. Paul R. Scheele, possibly the smartest person I know; and my dear friend Len Leritz, PhD, for always being willing to listen and encourage. Thank you so much.

Special thanks to my friends who helped me get here and to those I might have forgotten to put on this list. Irma Henson, Anne Engsig, Charlene Jones, Carol Gardner, Cheryl Schultz, Angela Quall, Mason Streeter, Ed Stansell, Jeffrey Smith, Ron Acierto, Bob Cramer, Allen Simmons, Mitzi Presnell, Cheryl Valk, Kathy VanRaden, Tiffany Windsor, and Ann Marsh, the best listener I have ever met. Hugs and kisses and much gratitude.

And last, but definitely not least, thank you to the hundreds of people who have shared their stories and dreams and frustrations with me and inspired me to write this book. You are truly amazing. I couldn't have done it without you.

ABOUT THE AUTHOR

Kathleen Sinclair is an environmentalist, animal lover, birder, and adventuress who has been on a mission for over fifteen years to reignite and inspire people over sixty to live a purpose-driven second half of life. She has worked with many authors and mentors, including Paul R. Scheele, PhD, Steven Kotler, Eric Edmeades, and Jack Canfield.

After sixty, she earned her master's degree, served in the Peace Corps for two years in Ukraine, and got certified in conflict resolution and mediation to work with the court system. Kathleen continues to roam the globe, promoting her unconventional ideas about living an encore life.

You can find her out in nature, reading a favorite mystery, and looking forward to getting a dog.

Made in the USA
Coppell, TX
20 November 2022

86747869R00146